MARXIST PERSPECTIVES ON IMPERIALISM

MARXIST PERSPECTIVES ON IMPERIALISM

A Theoretical Analysis

Chronis Polychroniou

PRAEGER

New York
Westport, Connecticut
London

Library of Congress Cataloging-in-Publication Data

Polychroniou, Chronis.
Marxist perspectives on imperialism : a theoretical analysis / Chronis Polychroniou.
p. cm.
Includes bibliographical references and index.
ISBN 0-275-93720-8
1. Marxian economics. 2. Dependency. 3. Imperialism. 4. Capitalism. I. Title.
HB97.5.P793 1991
335.4'1—dc20 90-45483

British Library Cataloguing in Publication Data is available.

Library of Congress Catalog Card Number: 90-45483
ISBN: 0-275-93720-8

First published in 1991

Praeger Publishers, One Madison Avenue, New York, NY 10010
An imprint of Greenwood Publishing Group, Inc.

Printed in the United States of America

The paper used in this book complies with the Permanent Paper Standard issued by the National Information Standards Organization (Z39.48-1984).

10 9 8 7 6 5 4 3 2 1

Copyright Acknowledgments

The author and publisher are grateful to the following for allowing the use of excerpts from:

Amin, Samir. *Unequal Development: An Essay on the Social Formulation of Peripheral Capitalism*. Copyright © 1976 by Monthly Review Press. Reprinted by permission of Monthly Review Foundation.

Amin, Samir. *Unequal Development: An Essay on the Social Formulation of Peripheral Capitalism*. Paris, France: Editions de minuit, 1976.

Amin, Samir. *Accumulations on a World Scale*. 2 vols. Copyright © 1974 by Monthly Review Press. Reprinted by permission of Monthly Review Foundation.

Amin, Samir. *Accumulations on a World Scale*. 2 vols. England, Harvest Wheatsheaf, 1974.

Arghiri, Emmanuel. *Unequal Exchange: A Study of the Imperialism of Trade*. Copyright © 1972 by Monthly Review Press. Reprinted by permission of Monthly Review Foundation.

Arghiri, Emmanuel. *Unequal Exchange: A Study of the Imperialism of Trade*. Paris, France: Editions la découverte, 1972.

Baran, Paul. *The Political Economy of Growth*. Copyright © 1957 by Monthly Review Press. Reprinted by permission of Monthly Review Foundation.

Blomstrom, Magnus, and Bjorn Hettne. *Development Theory in Transition*. London: Zed Books, 1984.

Hilferding, Rudolf. *Finance Capital*. London: Routledge & Kegan Paul, 1981.

Extract taken from *Imperialism: A Study* by J. A. Hobson, reproduced by kind permission of Unwin Hyman Ltd. Copyright © London, George Allen & Unwin, Ltd. 3rd revised edition 1954.

Laclau, Ernesto. "Feudalism and Capitalism in Latin America," in *Politics and Ideology in Marxist Theory*. London: New Left Books, 1977.

Lenin, V. I. "Imperialism: The Highest Stage of Capitalism." In *Selected Works*, vol. 1. New York: International Publishers, 1976.

Marx, Karl. *Capital*. 3 vols. New York: International Publishers, 1967.

Marx, Karl. *A Contribution to the Critique of Political Economy*, edited, with an introduction by Maurice Dobb. New York: International Publishers, 1970.

Marx, Karl, and Frederick Engels. *On Colonialism*. New York: International Publishers, 1972.

Marx, Karl, and Frederick Engels. "Manifesto of the Communist Party," in *Collected Works*, vol. 6. New York: International Publishers, 1976.

Palloix, Christian. "The Self-Expansion of Capital on a World Scale." *Review of Radical Political Economics* 9, no.2 (Summer 1977).

Warren, Bill. "Imperialism and Capitalist Industrialization." *New Left Review*, no. 81 (September-October 1973).

To Vicky

Contents

Figures and Tables

FIGURES

TABLES

Preface

This book presents a theoretical analysis of Marxist thought on the subject of capitalist imperialism. It seeks to provide a balanced treatment of the major Marxist perspectives on imperialism from the late nineteenth century to the present and to shed some light into the contours of the intellectual development of Marxism on international political economy. Its specific content, however, is not with the general history of Marxist thought on imperialism, but rather with its analytical foundations and theoretical dimensions. In a sense, then, this is an interpretative commentary. As such, this book is at once an analysis and a critique, concerned with theoretical propositions, methodological claims and premises and, yes, even ideological predispositions.

While the nature of the subject matter under consideration is both complex and diverse, I have tried to produce a book that is not very complicated. My intent has been to sharpen understanding of the way Marxist scholars have dealt with the phenomenon of capitalist imperialism and to assess their contributions. But I should like to stress that my goal is to provide a study that might benefit not only those already familiar with the field, but also those readers who are not. I have tried to produce a brief and readable account of Marxist writings on imperialism by attaching more importance to clarity and the need to outline and analyze the essential ideas contained in them, and less on the articulation of the specific discourse and the process of the formation of theoretically abstract terms and formulations—a characteristic feature of much of the Marxist literature. To this end I have found it also useful, if not necessary, to quote at length from original sources.

At the very heart of this book lies the conviction that Marxism remains as one of the most powerful conceptual frameworks for understanding and explaining social reality. As far as I can see, no other method or theory has had similar success in providing a systematic analysis of the socio-economic system of capitalism—the subject of much of the body of knowledge generated by Marxism. No doubt, since its inception as (a) a distinct method of analysis, and (b) a concrete, that is, a materialist and historically grounded theory of social development and change, Marxism has been on the whole able to grasp the inner dynamics of capitalism, to unmask its hidden contradictions, and—equally as important—to provide a frame of collective praxis for the radical transformation of capitalist social order and the making of a socialist world.

It goes without saying that, this conviction about the validity of Marxist analysis does not suggest in any possible way that all is well on the Marxist front. As it is, this book would not have been written at all if I thought so. For it was essentially a deep dissatisfaction with much of the post-World War II Marxist analyses on capitalist imperialism and the causes of underdevelopment in the Third World that prompted me to undertake this project. Moreover, one could not possibly overlook or deny the fact that Marxism finds itself, at the present historical "moment," in a state of crisis that, to put it mildly, is not merely theoretical or intellectual in nature and origin, but also political. The 1989 revolutionary upheavals in Eastern Europe and the ongoing processes of radical change and reconstruction in the Soviet Union have created without the slightest doubt much (although I believe unnecessary) confusion about the direction and future of Marxism. But at the same time it would be equally absurd to draw the conclusion that Marxism is, either as an intellectual tool or a political weapon, dead. Socialism is far from over. In fact, the collapse of Stalinism—a bureaucratic system based on brute political repression and ideological deception that fully abandoned the real goals and objectives of socialism—represents a world-historical transformation, that is, a profound historical turning point, which carries real opportunities for all progressive forces on the left, especially in the West. In the long run, no other factor was as much responsible for arresting the development of socialism as Stalinism itself. Thus for socialists worldwide, the end of Stalinism, as Samuel Bowels recently remarked, means "the end of a nightmare, not the death of a dream."[1]

Perhaps this is also the time when one has to remind that socialism sprang precisely as a reaction to capitalism. All this is another way of saying then that as long as the realities of the latter persist (social inequality, poverty, exploitation, and social injustice), so will the vision of the former (a society free of exploitation and class oppression). Indeed, I think that the pronouncement of the end of socialism—so deafening these days—has an outstanding chance of remaining an unrealized, frustrated expectation, a metaphysical expression of belief. At the same time, of course, there is little doubt that Marxists must turn almost immediately to the most pressing issues confronting socialism today: democracy and centralized planning. In any case, the eventual success of Marxism, it seems to me, depends almost entirely on its ability to come to terms with the nature of the new realities confronting today's world.

At this point I would like to thank some of the people who have been, either directly or indirectly, important to my intellectual development in general and the writing of this book in particular. While an undergraduate student, I derived much benefit from studying with Peter Bachrach (political science) and Joseph Margolis (philosophy) of Temple University; they enabled me to take seriously political theory and philosophical discourse. The late Nicos Poulantzas, though I met him only on a couple of occasions, and even though I do not agree with all of his analyses, was a major source of influence and inspiration in my pursuit of Marxist theory. There can be little doubt that he would have welcomed the historical changes occurring today around the world. There is also little doubt that he would have provided us with many useful and indeed much needed insights about the present historical juncture of socialism.

Initially the move toward this project was part of an effort to come to concrete terms with the *problematique* of imperialism. The emphasis shifted to the theme of Marxist studies on imperialism as part of an effort to come to concrete terms with the evolution and development of Marxist political economy. Indirectly, however, the interest on the subject of Marxist thought on imperialism arose gradually over the years as a result of numerous discussions, correspondence, and debates with personal friends and comrades concerning the ideological and strategic position of the socialist movement in the era of the internationalization of capital. I thank them for all the stimulation they have provided me with all these years; they know who they are.

In writing this book, I have received advice, comments, and fruitful suggestions from several individuals. I should like to thank James Oliver (political science), Gerald Turkel (sociology), Mark Miller (political science), and David Ingersoll (political science) of the University of Delaware. They were very generous with their time and expertise, and helped me at times in more ways than one.

I would also like to thank James Dunton, executive editor at Praeger, both for his helpful recommendations to improve this book, a well as for his overall interest and expeditiousness toward this project. Needless to say, of course, none of the aforementioned are in any way responsible for the views and interpretations expressed in this book.

Finally, I owe special thanks to Vicky Matsoglou-Polychroniou, who typed part of the manuscript, while offering at the same time unconditional support and understanding; and to Marie-Josèphe Descas, who spent much time with me during the late stages of this project raising pertinent questions in connection with the study of Marxism, as well as trying to remind me that there is more to life than Marxist theories of imperialism.

NOTE

1. Samuel Bowels, "Events in Eastern Europe Could Revitalize Leftist Scholarship," *Chronicle of Higher Education*, Vol. 36, No. 29 (April 4, 1990): A56.

Introduction

Imperialism is the hallmark of the twentieth century. The internationalization of capitalist economic life, which emerged at the turn of the century, has become a global trend and has produced far-reaching effects on the international system. In the twentieth century alone, inter-imperialist rivalries among the great capitalist countries have dragged humanity twice into global wars. In addition, the tendency toward the internationalization of economic life within the world capitalist system has produced at various times major economic catastrophes and corresponding differences in the economic development between the advanced capitalist countries and those of the Third World. Finally, imperialism has revealed its most ugly manifestations by continuously building weapons of awesome destructiveness that threaten the world with total extinction.

In view of these considerations, it is hardly surprising that Marxist scholars have made the question of imperialism the most pertinent one on their theoretical and empirical agenda. Of course, it is well known that the major Marxist figures of the early twentieth century—for example, Rudolf Hilferding, Rosa Luxemburg, Nikolai Bukharin, and V. I. Lenin—produced vital works on the question under consideration. But since the postwar period, the literature on Marxist studies of imperialism has grown to considerable proportions. Many political economists, historians, and sociologists from within the Marxist intellectual tradition have written at times about the nature, dynamics, and contradictions of contemporary capitalist expansion. Specifically, it is the impact of the interaction between the advanced capitalist countries and the social formations belonging to the so-called "Third World"—and in particular the problem of world inequalities and development—which serves as the principal focus of investigation for most of the postwar Marxist literature on capitalist imperialism. To be sure, the current predicament of the Third World has become the central concern of contemporary Marxist international political economy.

Still, despite the large proliferation of Marxist works on imperialism, there has yet to be developed a unified body of theory. Marxist thought is fraught with conflicting viewpoints and interpretations. Perhaps most importantly of all, neo-Marxist explanations of capitalist imperialism have been shaped by modes of thinking whose conceptual underpinnings are governed by a Third World*ist* perspective rather than class analysis. In fact, there is a serious dispute as to whether the most fashionable postwar Marxist theories of imperialism—for example, those of Paul Baran, Andre Gunder Frank, Immanuel Wallerstein, Arghiri Emmanuel, and Samir Amin—should be considered at all as part of the Marxist tradition. Indeed, there is a strong case that they are not to be made in favor of such an argument.

This work makes much of the contrast between traditional Marxist theory and what is known as neo-Marxism. In particular, it stresses that neo-Marxist interpretations of imperialism (dependency and world systems theory) bear a very superficial resemblance to the theoretical formulations and methodological approach of Marxism. (In a broader sense this work defends what some like to call *orthodox* or *fundamentalist* Marxism.) As shall be seen, in fact, the authors in this tradition employ a methodology for explaining international political economy that is, in many respects, pre-Marxist in nature and origin. In this sense, neo-Marxist analyses on imperialism have failed not only to explain the essence and the causes of capitalist expansion, but have actually hindered the further development of Marxian international political economy.

What follows here does not constitute a review or general survey of the Marxist literature on imperialism. Many important contributions have in fact been left out. This is not only because such undertakings already exist,[1] but also because this study has a rather specific aim: namely, to put into proper perspective the differences between the classical Marxist and the neo-Marxist approaches to imperialism. With this in view, Chapter 1 outlines the method of historical materialism and presents an exposition of Marx's analysis of the capitalist mode of production as well as his views on the nature and impact of capitalist expansion. This chapter intends to serve as the background for evaluating the analyses of classical Marxist and neo-Marxist perspectives on imperialism.

Chapter 2 reviews the studies of the classical Marxist theoreticians on imperialism: Hilferding, Luxemburg, Bukharin, and Lenin. Also included in this discussion is John Atkinson Hobson's work on imperialism. The inclusion of Hobson in a study devoted to Marxist theories of imperialism was motivated by the desire to show that, contrary to what is often claimed, his theoretical framework remained firmly rooted in the liberal tradition, and did not therefore serve in any way as the basis for Lenin's own formulations on the question of imperialism.

Chapter 3 examines the major and most influential neo-Marxist theories of imperialism. It will be shown here that the analyses of Baran, Frank, Wallerstein, Emmanuel, and Amin are based on a methodology which, despite claims by some of these theorists to the contrary, constitutes a clear break with the basic tenets of the Marxian method of analysis. This critique is intended to provide an analytical exegesis of the essential premises of the neo-Marxist approach as well as a theoretical exposition of its main weaknesses.

Finally, Chapter 4 discusses various current attempts to analyze and explain imperialism from a more orthodox Marxist viewpoint. More specifically, the attention is focused on the work of Bill Warren, the modes of production approach, and the internationalization of capital. A brief conclusion summarizes the main arguments and analysis presented in this work.

NOTE

1. A number of volumes have been published in recent years that aim at presenting a broad survey of the Marxist literature on imperialism. Among the more important studies are the following: Anthony Brewer, *Marxist Theories of Imperialism: A Critical Survey* (London: Routledge and Kegan Paul, 1980); and Charles A. Barone, *Marxist Thought on Imperialism: Survey and Critique* (Armonk, NY: M. E. Sharpe, 1985). Both of these works have been very useful to my own analysis.

1

Marxian Political Economy: Methodological and Theoretical Foundations

Marxian political economy employs a conceptual approach, both in terms of its methodological guidelines and theoretical analysis, which is unique among the social sciences. Its uniqueness rests on two interrelated foundations: first, the formulation and determination of capitalist economic relations, concepts, and categories are grounded in a "materialist conception of history;" and, second, a systematic focus on unifying theory and praxis. As such, Marxian political economy is both a scientific and revolutionary science. It is scientific because Marx's study of the socio-economic system of capitalism analyzes the underlying nature of this system and explains how it works. It is also revolutionary in that its concepts are formed through a totalizing critique of capitalism. Marx's approach systematically and consciously paves the way for practical strategies that would lead to the eventual establishment of a social order emancipating the real needs and aspirations of humanity.[1]

In its general conception Marxian political economy studies the production relations of society and their interconnection with the development of the productive forces. Its focus of investigation, unlike with conventional economics, centers not on things, but rather on relations between people, and, more fundamentally, between classes.

Marx himself saw his aim as the scientific study of the capitalist mode of production. He stressed that bourgeois political economy was incapable of studying capitalism scientifically. In his view, this was because the classical bourgeois economists held an ahistorical conception of capitalism:

> Economists express the relations of bourgeois production, the division of labor, credit, money, etc., as fixed, immutable, eternal categories. . . . Economists explain how production takes place in the above-mentioned relations, but what they do not explain is how these relations themselves are produced, that is, the historical moment which gave them birth . . . these categories are as little eternal as the relations they express. They are historical and transitory products.[2]

Indeed, according to Marx, the character of bourgeois political economy is constituted on the basis of a methodological outlook in which "the capitalist regime is looked upon as the absolutely final form of social production, instead of a passing historical phase of its evolution."[3]

In contrast, Marx's economic analysis of capitalism is firmly grounded in a socio-historical approach. Having recognized that economic principles and categories "bear the stamp of history,"[4] Marx demonstrated that capitalist economic relations have an historical character, expressing the nature of the specific productive relations of the capitalist mode of production. Capitalism is not conceptualized as a natural and eternal phenomenon, removed from any historical context, but the result of a process determined by "the real and the concrete."[5]

Marxian political economy was the result of the culmination of an effort to gain an understanding of the dynamics of history, that is, of the whole historical process leading to the emergence and the evolution of the capitalist social formation. Marx insisted that the conceptual construction and articulation of specific modes of production and social formations can be carried out successfully only within the domain of historical totality.[6] This line of methodological reasoning stems from Marx's notion that humanity creates itself in an historical process and that, as such, in the real constructive effort to understand and analyze social reality, history holds the key to the success of such an endeavor. Indeed, Marx undertook his critical study of political economy with the premise that "We know only a single science, the science of history."[7]

For these reasons, it is appropriate that we discuss the main tenets of Marx's theory of history before presenting the subject-matter of Marxian political economy.

HISTORICAL MATERIALISM

Marx and, to a lesser extent, Engels developed a theory of history, known as "the materialist conception of history" (or, historical materialism). This approach, rooted in a dialectical conception of reality, which revolved around the idea that every thing contains not only itself but also its opposite, sought to systematically define the patterns of social and historical development and the nature and character of social structures in various social formations. Nicos Poulantzas has summarized the concept of historical materialism well:

> Historical materialism (the science of history) has as its object the concept of history, through the study of the various modes of production and social formations, their structure, constitution and functioning, and the forms of transition from one social formation to another.[8]

The materialist conception of history maintains that history and social development are rooted in material conditions of life. This is opposed to idealist interpretations of history and, more directly, the Hegelian view, which take "ideas" and "consciousness" to be the directive forces in the determination of the evolution of history. Marx argued that the "historical" is a category defined by specific relations between the productive forces of society and the relations of production, on the one hand, and governed by the agency of class conflict and struggles on the other. In this perspective, history is not the development of ideas but, rather, the result and product of social interventions. Historical developments, according to Marx, take place in a definite social sphere of activities and correspond to the conditions of the production process. Marx argued that human consciousness originates in existing social reality. Accordingly, social change is an objective development stemming from the real contradictions encountered in the complex relations of a given social formation. Marx formulated the conceptual framework of the materialist conception of history most directly in his famous 1859 Preface to *A Contribution to the Critique of Political Economy*.

> The general conclusion at which I arrived and which, once reached, became the guiding principles of my studies can be summarized as follows. In the social production of their existence, men inevitably enter into definite relations, which are independent of their will, namely relations of production appropriate to a given stage in the development of their material forces of production. The totality of these relations of production constitutes the economic structure of society, the real foundation, on which arises a legal and political superstructure and to which correspond definite forms of social consciousness. The mode of production of material life conditions the general process of social, political and intellectual life. It is not the consciousness of men that determines their existence, but their social existence that determines their consciousness.
>
> At a certain stage of development, the material productive forces of society come into conflict with the existing relations of production or—this merely expresses the same thing in legal terms—with the property relations within the framework of which they have operated hitherto. From forms of development of the productive forces these relations turn into their fetters. Then begins an era of social revolution. The changes in the economic foundation lead sooner or later to the transformation of the whole immense superstructure.

> In studying such transformations it is always necessary to distinguish between the material transformation of the economic conditions of production, which can be determined with the precision of natural science, and the legal, political, religious, artistic or philosophic—in short, ideological forms in which men become conscious of this conflict and fight it out. Just as one does not judge an individual by what he thinks about himself, so one cannot judge such a period of transformation by its consciousness, but, on the contrary, this consciousness must be explained from the contradictions of material life, from the conflict existing between the social forces of production and the relations of production.[9]

Marx's conceptual framework of the materialist conception of history, as expressed in the passage cited above, represents a sweeping formulation of the sum of collections and relationships in the structural process of the development of society and history. The basic terms and principles in the materialist conception of history are neither well elaborated nor are they adequately grounded in the context of a specific theoretico-analytical framework.[10] Moreover, it is indeed true that "no formal exposition of historical materialism was ever published by Marx himself."[11] As a result Marx's theory of history has remained ambiguous and, therefore, open to a variety of interpretations and theoretical projects. In the absence of a systematic effort to attain an understanding of the principles of historical materialism from the standpoint of an interpretive perspective corresponding substantively within the scope and dimensions of Marx's methodological guidelines and theoretical analyses, Marx's theory of history can be easily transformed into a "mechanical formula" which explains everything by explaining nothing. Indeed this is the case with those interpretations that argue that Marx's theory of history is evolutionary or represents yet another form of technological determinism.[12]

The formulation of historical materialism given by Marx in the 1859 Preface constitutes a complex problematic that is expressed through abstract concepts. It is not, however, a mechanical conception of the dynamics of history and social development. Rather, human practice plays a crucial role in Marx's theory of history. Moreover, Marx's theory of history is firmly grounded in the specifics of history. Far from being formal conceptualizations, the theoretical formulations encountered in Marx's theory of history represent an area of discourse which corresponds to the direction of the investigation of definite theoretical problems. Marx's numerous historical and political writings demonstrate that. This, however, does not mean that Marxism is mere historiography.

For Marx, theoretical concepts are produced through a synthesis of "many determinations."[13] Concrete problems are appropriated through a specific process of abstraction. This process of abstraction assimilates the concrete "and reproduces it as a concrete mental category."[14] Ultimately, by comprehending the relationship of the specifics of history with the totality of social reality one can penetrate and expose the dynamic forces of history. Thus, in *The German Ideology* Marx and Engels observed that the conception and articulation of the historical process

> relies on expounding the real process of production—starting from the material production of life itself—and comprehending the form of intercourse connected with and created by this mode of production, i.e., civil society in its various stages, as the basis of all history; describing it in its action as the state, and also explaining how all the different theoretical products and forms of consciousness, religion, philosophy, morality, etc., etc., arise from it, and tracing the process of their formation from that basis; thus the whole thing can, of course, be depicted in its totality (and therefore, too, the reciprocal action of these various sides on one another).[15]

Marx's aim was to grasp the complexity of social reality in its totality. In this respect Marx concluded that it was necessary to develop a conceptual framework which would serve as a guide toward that goal. More important, this conceptual framework, if it was to be scientific, had to be couched both in logical and historical terms. It would require the explanatory power to reconstitute the concrete within the reflection of the abstract.

Stated differently, the method of historical materialism suggests that "each specific phenomenon must be examined individually, but without the knowledge of the general phenomenon of which it is part, specific analysis has no basis."[16] Engels captured the essence of this idea when he wrote that,

> Our conception of history is above all a guide. . . . All history must be studied afresh, the conditions of existence of the different formations of society must be individually examined before the attempt is made to deduce from them the political, civil-legal, aesthetic, philosophic, religious, etc., notions corresponding to them.[17]

Thus, Marx's method of analysis combines an epistemological and methodological posture which precludes a reductionist conception of history and society. In this sense, Marx's 1859 Preface would have caused far fewer problems if it were seen as nothing more than "the form of exposition proper to a scientific analysis."[18] Indeed, as Derek Sayer has recently reemphasized, "general formulations of the kind found in the 1859 Preface should be treated as exactly what Marx said they were—precisely a 'guiding thread,' an orientation to empirical and historical research, not a theoretical substitute for it."[19]

Let us now discuss the basic tenets of historical materialism. The real processes of the material conditions of life must serve as the starting point for our understanding of history and social development. In this context, the production process is at the center of social life and reveals itself as the constitutive and directing force in the sphere of social relations. This is a rather simple idea, but it needs to be further explained because of its overall importance in Marx's approach to the study and comprehension of historical developments and social change.

Production and the production process are specific social and historical phenomena. Production is essential to the maintenance and the development of society. No society can exist and maintain itself if it does not produce and reproduce the necessary means of life. Consequently production is a social relation since it involves human activities and social organization. Furthermore, the form and content of production are stipulated, in the final analysis, by the historical conditions in which production occurs. The production process never remains static or fixed; it is always subject to develop and change. Hence as the productive forces within a given society change, so does the production process itself.

The productive forces include the means and tools that are available at a given time. These are used to produce and reproduce the means of subsistence. More specifically, the productive forces include tools, science, technology, knowledge, skills, human activity, and modes of cooperation. (For Marx, production as a process involves four essential elements: work, the subject of that work, instruments, and cooperation). In other words, the productive forces are not merely those technical elements used in the production process; on the contrary, they entail social aspects as well. It is indeed a mistake to consider the productive forces in a reductionist way and assume in a fashion similar to that of Marxist technological determinism that "to qualify as a productive force, a facility must be capable of use by a producing agent in such a way that production occurs (partly) as a result of its use, and it is someone's purpose that the facility so constitute to production."[20] In the context of such an interpretation, work relations are excluded from the productive forces.[21] But Marx and Engels certainly thought otherwise when they stated in *The German Ideology* that "a certain mode of production . . . is always combined with a certain mode of cooperation, or social stage, and this mode of cooperation is itself a 'productive force.'"[22]

At the same time Marx recognized that productive forces of society are not neutral for the pattern of social organization. Rather, productive forces have significant repercussions on the way people produce and exchange the means of life. The definition of property relations, for example, and the way people relate to one another are conditioned by the existing productive forces of society. Productive forces affect the social relations of production. The material forces of production determine the pattern of labor organization in the production process.

In one not unsubstantial sense, the relations of production constitute the structure of class relations in a given society. Consequently it is through the structure of class relations that we can define a society's mode of production.[23] In the case of capitalism, for example, the capitalist mode of production is characterized by the specific relation between the worker and the capitalist. Under capitalism, the capitalist owns the means of production; on the other hand, the worker owns nothing but his ability to sell his labor power for wages. However, it is important to note here that it is possible within a given society to encounter more than one mode of production. But there is always one dominant mode of production, and it is the contradictions mainly within the dominant mode of production that create class conflicts and social crises.

Class production relations have existed throughout recorded history.[24] The slave mode of production, feudalism, and capitalism were based on production relations characterized by the division of each respective social formation into classes. Further, each class-divided society, whether it be that of the slave mode of production, feudalism, or capitalism, embodies two essential and antagonistic classes. As Nikolai Bukharin put it,

> on the one hand, the class which commands, monopolizing the instruments of production; on the other hand, the executing class, with no means of production, which works for the former. The specific form of this relation of economic exploitation and servitude determines the form of the given

> class society. For example, if the relation between the commanding and executing class is reproduced by the purchase of labor power in the market, we have capitalism. If it is reproduced by the purchase of persons, by plunder, or otherwise, and if the commanding class gains control of not only the labor power but also of body and soul of the exploited persons, we have a slaveholding system, etc.[25]

Marx analyzed the capitalist mode of production as the last historical form of class organization. The implication is that capitalism is objectively laying the foundations for the emergence of a "cooperative society" through its ability to enhance the growth of productive forces in a way that provides for a massive increase in the material conditions of life and, with it, an end to the exploitation of man by man. With the spread of capitalism, therefore, society is provided with the necessary material conditions for human emancipation.

Human emancipation, however, under capitalism is impossible. Capitalism is a system, after all, based on exploitation and the domination of a minority class over the majority of people. Indeed, Marx expected that once it had fulfilled its historic mission, capitalism would be overthrown and replaced in turn by a new, more rational and humane, social order. That is to say that while for Marx capitalism plays on the one hand a progressive role in the movement of history by having created "more massive and more colossal productive forces than have all preceding generations together,"[26] it is vested on the other hand with many contradictions, which by their very nature are bound to generate crises of the capitalist socio-economic order. Marx depicted this notion in his famous discussion of the "historical tendency of capitalist accumulation." He wrote:

> Along with the constantly diminishing number of the magnates of capital, who usurp and monopolize all advantages of this process of transformation, grows the mass of misery, oppression, slavery, degradation, exploitation; but with this

> too grows the revolt of the working class, a class always increasing in numbers, and disciplined, united, organized by the very mechanism of the process of capitalist production itself. The monopoly of capital becomes a fetter upon the mode of production. Centralization of the means of production and socialization of labor at last reach a point where they become incompatible with their capitalist integument. Thus integument is burst asunder. The knell of capitalist private property sounds. The expropriators are expropriated.[27]

This passage underscores Marx's firm view that the internal contradictions of capitalism would eventually lead to the system's downfall. But it does not in any way presuppose that the collapse of capitalism will take place on its own. While the contradictions of capitalism certainly undermine the foundations of the whole system, its transformation rests ultimately upon the active intervention of the working class; capitalism will not transform itself but must be overthrown by the working class. With the active overthrow of capitalism and the creation of socialist social relations, private property would be eliminated and the means of production would be appropriated and owned of the whole society. At this stage of social development, the division of society into classes would gradually disappear, thereby slowly giving rise to the last historical stage in production relations, that is, communism. This is a society, as Marx and Engels declared, "in which the free development of each is the condition for the free development of all."[28]

In Marx's materialist conception of history, society is divided into two major components: the economic structure and the legal and political superstructure. The productive forces and the relations of production constitute the economic structure of society. With the development of the economic structure, however, a political superstructure emerges, that is, a state, a legal system, an ideological system, norms, values, etc. The political superstructure maintains and defends the economic structure of society.

The state and its apparatuses, for example, represent the interests of the dominant economic classes within a given society. The state represents those interests, either in the short or long run, by reflecting the logic of the economic system and the urgent need to strengthen and reproduce the existing social relations. By its very nature the state is the material power of the ruling class. From this perspective the superstructure in general, and the state in particular, is not an autonomous entity. But this does not mean that it lacks the ability to influence and effect the underlying economic structure of society. At times the state acts quite independently, without specific reference to the interests of the most dominant economic classes.[29] However, in the last instance, the state is always determined by the economic structure.

Having considered the conception of structural relations and contradictions, what are the processes of social change in Marx's historical materialism? The dynamics of social change manifest themselves at two interrelated levels. At one level, historical change takes place with the development of the productive forces. As the productive forces of society develop, they eventually come into direct conflict with the existing relations of production. This contradictory development initiates a transition from one social order to another social order, which is qualitatively and quantitatively different from the previous one. Such was the case, for example, with the transition to capitalism from feudalism. However, the completion of the transitional stage from one social order to a new order is accomplished only as a result of the active intervention of social classes in the process of class struggle. As we havé pointed out, class struggle is an active element in social development, even though its form and content are conditioned by objective processes of a given socio-economic formation. In *The Eighteenth Brumaire of Louis Bonaparte*, Marx stressed that "men make their own history, but they do not make it just as they please; they do not make it under circumstances chosen by themselves, but under circumstances directly encountered, given and transmitted from the past."[30]

While Marx emphasized the contradiction between productive forces and relations of production as the objective factor in the course of social development, he argued that class struggle is "the motif force of history." In *The Manifesto of the Communist Party*, Marx and Engels categorically stated that

> the history of all hitherto existing society is the history of class struggles. Freeman and slave, patrician and plebeian, lord and serf, guild-master and journeyman, in a word, oppressor and oppressed, stood in constant opposition to one another, carried on an uninterrupted, now hidden, now open fight, a fight that each time ended, either in a revolutionary reconstitution of society at large, or in the common ruin of the contending classes.[31]

Against this backdrop of the role of the class struggle in the course of human history, it is quite misleading to describe Marx's theory as a technologically deterministic view of history and social development. Historical materialism must be understood in terms of both the objective developments within a given social formation and the active intervention of the agency of the class struggle. Finally, historical materialism is not a general theory of history. Marx sought to explain historical developments in Western Europe.[32] When he discussed non-European societies, he took a different course of analysis than the one he used to explain the development in Western Europe, that is, the "Asiatic mode of production."[33] Yet, more often than not, Marxist scholars pay allegiance to a dogmatic interpretation of historical materialism, thereby asserting that Marx's theory of history is a theory of "a universal law of development."[34] However, Marx did not have a unilinear or "universal" theory of historical development. Indeed, in reaction to such an interpretation of his analytical method by a reviewer of *Das Kapital*, Marx responded:

> The chapter on primitive accumulation does not pretend to do more than trace the path by which, in Western Europe,

> the capitalist order of economy emerged from the womb of the feudal order of economy. It therefore describes the historic movement which by divorcing the producers from their means of production converts them into wage earners (proletarians in the modern sense of the word) while it converts into capitalists those who hold the means of production in possession.
>
> But that is not enough for my critic. He feels himself obliged to metamorphose my historical sketch of the genesis of capitalism in Western Europe into an historico-philosophic theory of the marche generale (general path) imposed by fate upon people, whatever the historical circumstances in which it finds itself, in order that it may ultimately arrive at the form of economy which will ensure, together with the greatest expansion of the productive powers of social labor, the most complete development of man. But I beg his pardon. (He is both honouring and shaming me too much.)[35]

It was Marx's view that the method of historical materialism is not to be utilized, if it is to retain any explanatory value, in a reductionist manner, as if its epistemological premises involve nothing more than deductive abstraction from the general principles of an all-embracing philosophical system. Historical materialism, removed from concrete analysis and interpretative contexts, runs the danger of collapsing into the realm of metaphysics. Failure to understand this means a failure to understand how Marx succeeded not only to challenge openly and explicitly the methodology of bourgeois political economy, but also to disclose the operations of the capitalism system itself.

THE ANALYSIS OF THE CAPITALIST MODE OF PRODUCTION

The task of discovering the inner nature of the capitalist economic system was Marx's central intellectual pursuit. Beginning with his reading of Engels's *Outlines of a Critique of Political*

Economy (1844), Marx became convinced that only through political economy could bourgeois society be understood and properly analyzed. On the other hand, Marx's politico-economic project took many forms and developments before it assumed its complete and scientific character in the first volume of *Das Kapital* in 1867. Up to that point, Marx's economic studies of capitalism remained either fragmentary or were heavily preconditioned by philosophical pronouncements whose ontological foundations may have indeed undermined the character of the inquiry itself. To be sure, such works as the *Economic and Philosophic Manuscripts, The Poverty of Philosophy*, and certainly the *Grundrisse* remain important works, especially since they clarified Marx's methodology. Yet it is the first, second, and third volume of *Das Kapital* that provides us, both methodologically and theoretically, with the overall framework of Marx's political economy. For this reason, the following discussion of Marx's analysis of the capitalist mode of production is based, for the most part, on those principles and insights provided to us through the pages of the *Das Kapital*.

For Marx, capitalism represents a specific, historically determined mode of production which is characterized by (a) the monopolization of the means of production into the hands of a small minority, while the large minority of people is forced to sell its labor power in order to survive, and (b) the designation of a production process centered around the pursuit of profit. Historically, capitalism represents the most advanced form of commodity production. The production of commodities intended for sale, instead of consumption by its immediate producers, constitutes the system's overall defining characteristic. Unlike petty commodity production, whereby both the products of labor and the means of production belonged exclusively to the producers themselves, capitalist production is distinguished by "that stage of the development of commodity production at which not only the producers of human labor, but human labor-power itself becomes a commodity."[36] As such, the extraction of profit (or the generation of surplus value), as we shall see later, becomes the driving force of the capitalist commodity production in which exploitation is a necessity.

In the opening pages of *Das Kapital* Marx observes that "the wealth of those societies in which the capitalist mode of production prevails presents itself as 'an immense accumulation of commodities,' its unit being a single commodity."[37] For Marx, the analysis of capitalism should begin with an analysis into the nature of commodities, and not with the structural formation of the system as a whole. This is consistent with Marx's materialist method to begin with an inquiry based on the most basic and fundamental concepts, in this case commodities, as a way of discovering the inner structure and logic of a social process.

A commodity is any product of labor that is produced for sale on the market and for exchange with another commodity. This means that commodities possess not only use-value, in that they satisfy human needs, but also exchange-value. Exchange-value signifies the quantitative ratio of exchanged commodities. However, while all commodities possess use-value, there are many useful things which do not possess exchange-value and, therefore, can never take the form of commodities. Such is the case, for example, with air. In order, then, for a commodity to be exchanged it must possess both exchange-value and use-value.

In addition, for exchange to be possible, all commodities must contain some common substance. This common substance that allows a quantitative comparison to be made between different commodities is their value, that is, the fact that they are products of human labor. There can be no value without use-value. Thus, air possesses use-value without possessing value. As such, any article of use-value has value only because human labor has been embodied in it.

The value of a commodity is determined by the quantity of the socially necessary labor time that is "required to produce an article under the normal conditions of production, and with the average degree of skill and intensity prevalent at the time."[38] This is better known as the Labor Theory of Value, and it constitutes the foundation of Marxian political economy. The main purpose of the Labor Theory of Value is to penetrate and ultimately determine the mechanism which governs capitalist economic relations. In this sense, its task is to provide the basis for an understanding of the phenomenon of exploitation under capitalism.

Marx's formulation of the Labor Theory of Value is underlined by his critique of classical political economy. Classical political economy managed to discover that the value of commodities is determined by the labor embodied in them. Nonetheless, it "never once asked the question why labor is represented by the value of its product and labor-time by the magnitude of that value."[39] This is to say that, because of its view of commodity as a natural phenomenon, classical political economy was unable to recognize that a product of labor becomes a commodity precisely "at the epoch when the labor spent on the production of a useful article becomes expressed as one of the objective qualities of that article, i.e., as its value."[40] By failing to distinguish between labor and labor power, classical political economy had a difficult time explaining the determination of wages, let alone dealing with the question of the contradictions of capitalism.

The key to Marx's Labor Theory of Value is that value is a social relationship. Value is an objective economic category, operating exclusively in the context and on the basis of capitalist commodity production, and underlies the specific form of relationships between labor and capital.[41] Under capitalism, human labor and production are allocated and carried out in conditions marked by the private ownership of the means of production, on the one hand, and regulated by the imperatives of competition on the other. As such, capitalist economy and society functions in the absence of a conscious social regulation of production. Competition and anarchy reign supreme in capitalist social organization. Nevertheless, each producer does not stand in total isolation from the social whole. The law of value renders the private labor of individuals into socialized labor the moment the act of the exchange of products in the market as commodities takes place. (In other words, labor becomes a representation of value in the sphere of social exchange.) Labor, as the substance of value, serves as the common denominator for the exchange of products, since products differ from one another. Thus, given the nature and character of capitalist production, the abstract equalization of labor assures a relationship of organized exchanges.[42]

For Marx, value is the abstract labor time embodied in commodity.[43] Here abstract labor refers to the generalized expenditure of human effort, energy, and labor that is the ground for equivalence of exchange. On the other hand, labor that is used to produce use-values refers to concrete labor. This distinction between concrete and abstract labor stems from the dual nature of a commodity, that is, from the distinction between use-value and exchange-value. However, the concept of abstract labor is not a mere mental construct but, as we have already seen, "the basic common denominator of labor upon which relative value ratios are based."[44] In this sense, abstract labor is in essence a "hidden" form of social labor. Indeed, the realization of abstract labor as part of the aggregate total of social labor becomes evident only on the market, that is, through the act of exchange. Thus, in exchange, as Marx wrote, "concrete labor becomes the form under which its opposite, abstract human labor manifests itself."[45]

Value and labor become more abstract the greater the extent of commodity production and exchange. In the early historical stages of commodity production, when exchange was still accidental in nature, the value of one commodity was realized by virtue of its exchange relationship with another commodity. However, with the further development of commodity production, which necessarily introduced a sharper social division of labor, and the rise of money, the value of a commodity was expressed in the form of prices. Money, in other words, functioned now as a measure of value and, subsequently, as a medium in the circulation of commodities. In the light of this development, the exchange of commodities (*C-C*) took now the form of the exchange of commodities through money(*C-M-C*). But the historical process of the development of commodity production does not stop here. At a certain historical moment, money, especially when it begins to operate beyond national boundaries, that is, when it becomes world money, is transformed into capital. The transformation of money into capital, which occurs essentially as a result of the utilization of the various levels of values, is expressed in the formula: *M-C-M'*. The *M-C-M'* formula is the general formula of capital, and simply states that the owner of money buys in order to sell over the value originally advanced. Thus capital is nothing short of self-expanding value, that is, value that generates surplus value. Marx defined surplus value as follows:

> The exact form of this process is therefore *M-C-M'*, where $M' = M + \Delta M$ = the original sum advanced, plus an increment. This increment or excess over the original value I call "surplus value." The value originally advanced, therefore, not only remains intact while in circulation, but adds to itself a surplus value or expands itself. It is this movement that converts it into capital.[46]

Nonetheless, there is a basic contradiction in the general formula of capital. The circuit *M-C-M'*, which refers to merchants' capital, is a movement, as Marx pointed out, "that takes place entirely within the sphere of circulation."[47] Hence the question arises as to where surplus value comes from. Surplus value cannot possibly be created from commodity circulation, for the process of circulation is an exchange of equivalents. If commodities of equal value are exchanged, the circuit *M-C-M'* becomes *M-C-M*. Thus, "it is therefore impossible for capital to be produced by circulation, and it is equally impossible for it to originate apart from circulation. It must have its origin both in circulation and yet not in circulation."[48] Based on this insight, Marx demonstrated that while surplus value is indeed realized in the sphere of circulation, its creation must occur elsewhere, namely in the production process.

The production of surplus value is the fundamental economic law of capitalism. Capitalist production has as its objective aim and goal not the production of use-values as such, but rather that of surplus value. The production of surplus value is realized in essence as a result of the ability of the capitalist to buy in the market some commodity whose "use-value possesses the peculiar property of being the source of value."[49] This special commodity is none other than labor power.

Labor power, defined by Marx as "the aggregate of those mental and physical capabilities existing in a human being, which he exercises whenever he produces a use-value of any description,"[50] has existed of course in every society. But labor power offered as a commodity for sale, like any other commodity of use-value, is specific to capitalist commodity production. This is because in order for labor power to become a commodity it is imperative that the workers be turned into *free workers* in a double sense. First, they must possess the legal right to freely sell their labor power; that is, they cannot be, as in pre-capitalist societies, slaves or serfs. And, second, they must be deprived, that is, "free," of the ownership of the means of production, so that they would have no alternative but to sell their labor power in order to support themselves. From this point of view, as Marx stated, the condition of labor under capitalism "has no natural basis, neither is its social basis one that is common to all historical periods. It is clearly the result of a past historical development, the product of many economic revolutions, of the extinction of a whole series of older forms of social production."[51]

The value of labor power as a commodity, like that of any other commodity, is determined by the labor time socially necessary for its production and reproduction. In other words, the value of labor power corresponds with the physiological and social needs necessary for the subsistence of the worker and the reproduction of labor power. With this qualification, it follows that wages must change in proportion to the overall needs of workers in a given socio-historical period. Nevertheless, "wages," as Marx stated, "are a converted form of the value or price of labor power."[52]

Wages mask the reality that workers receive less than the actual amount of labor that they perform. As Marx pointed out:

> As the value of labor is only an irrational expression for the value of labor power, it follows, of course, that the value of labor must always be less than the value it produces, for the capitalist always makes labor power work longer than is necessary for the reproduction of its own value.[53]

Under capitalism, the workers create new value which is greater than the value of their labor power. This is the essence of surplus value, and the core of the exploitation of the worker by the capitalist.

For Marxian political economy, surplus value is created in the sphere of the production process and by labor alone. Marx captured this in the following way:

$$M - C\begin{cases} Lp \\ Mp \end{cases} \ldots\ldots P \ldots\ldots C'\ (C+c) - M'\ (M+m)$$

This formula briefly describes the movement of capital through three consecutive stages. In the first stage, the capitalist appears on the commodity and labor market with his money (*M*), where he buys the commodities (*C*), that is, the means of production (*Mp*) and labor power (*Lp*), needed in the production process. In this context, his money is transformed now into productive capital. In the second stage, his capital penetrates the sphere of the production process (....*P*....), which results in the creation of a commodity (*C′*) with more value than that of the commodities (*C*) originally entered into production. Now productive capital has been transformed into commodity-capital. In the third stage, the capitalist returns to the commodity market and sells the commodities produced for money (*C′ - M′*). Thus *C′* reflects the production of surplus value, while *M′* the realization of surplus value. Commodity-capital is now transformed into augmented money capital.

Accordingly, direct labor alone creates surplus value. Neither exchange, as we have seen, nor machines (indirect labor) can create surplus value. Machines cannot create surplus value for the mere fact that they cannot be exploited by the capitalist. For example, in buying machinery, as well as in the case of raw materials, the capitalist, with the exception of cheating and underpricing, must pay for the full value of these commodities, since they are sold to him by another capitalist. Thus, while these commodities possess value, they cannot create surplus value. This leaves labor power as the only source available for the extraction of surplus value. Thus, as Meghnad Desai writes, "in the case of labor alone, due to the unequal nature of social relations, there is a gap between use-value and exchange value of labor power. At the end of each productive process the laborer reproduces himself and the capitalist accumulates wealth."[54]

DYNAMICS AND CONTRADICTIONS IN THE ACCUMULATION PROCESS

Capitalist accumulation is the conversion of surplus value into capital for the purpose of producing more surplus value. Moreover, capital is a social relation, specific to the capitalist mode of production, which is based on the exploitation of wage labor:

> Capital is not a thing, but rather a definite social production relation belonging to a definite historical formation of society, which is manifested in a thing and lends this thing a specific social character. Capital is not the sum of the material and produced means of production. Capital is rather the means of production transformed into capital, which in themselves are no more capital than gold or silver in itself is money. It is the means of production monopolized by a certain section of society, confronting living labor power as products and working conditions rendered independent of this very labor power, which are personified through this antithesis in capital.[55]

The accumulation of capital is an objective movement and develops on the basis of the appropriation of unpaid labor power. From an historical point, the scale of accumulation depends on the specific form of the expansion of capital and on the productive power of social labor. Hence when capital expansion faces itself with a low organic composition of capital, the increase of capital is actualized by the growth in absolute surplus value. This implies, of course, the lengthening of the workday and the reduction in real wage. Eventually, absolute surplus value is supplemented with relative surplus value when the organic composition of capital has risen, which reflects in itself a rise in the productivity of labor.

Under competitive conditions, the drive to maximize profit among discrete blocs of capital compels all capitalists to improve productivity—a process which results in the rise of the organic composition of capital, thereby leading to an equalization of the rate of profit across industrial branches of the economy. However, the structural accumulation of capital also results in a large surplus of labor power, thereby creating an industrial reserve army of labor. Competition also causes the ruin of small capitalists. To be sure, capitalist accumulation is an anarchic and contradictory process. The logic of the accumulation of capital leads to enormous wealth, on the one hand, and the relative impoverishment of the working class on the other:

> The greater the social wealth, the functioning of capital, the extent and energy of its growth, and, therefore, also the absolute mass of the proletariat and the productiveness of its labor, the greater is the industrial reserve army. The same causes which develop the expansive power of capital, develop also the labor power at its disposal. The relative mass of the industrial reserve army increases therefore with the potential energy of wealth.[56]

At the same time, the manifold activities of capitalist accumulation also accelerate the process of the concentration and centralization of capital, and indeed of the transformation of competitive capitalism into monopoly capitalism in general. Concentration and centralization of capital are interdependent processes partially created through competition.[57] Nevertheless, centralization does not eliminate competition. No matter how highly concentrated and centralized capital becomes, the existence of competition remains firm and continues to serve as the driving force over the expansion and appropriation of surplus value. In this sense, competition is not to be confused with the conditions and forces of the market; that is, competition cannot be identified in terms of the actual number of existing individual capitals at any given time—a point very much ignored by many modern Marxist writers. Nor is it to be understood in a fashion identical with the principles of perfect competition in the classical or neoclassical sense. "Conceptually," as Marx pointed out, "*competition* is nothing other than the inner *nature of capital*, its essential character, appearing in and realized as the reciprocal interaction of many capitals with one another, the inner tendency as external necessity."[58] In short, competition is a dynamic element which accelerates the growth of monopolies by virtue of the fact that, as Marx put it, "one capitalist always kills many."[59] Yet this process in no way signifies the negation of competition; for, in the final analysis, "capital exists and can only exist as many capitals. . . ."[60]

According to Marx, however, along with the processes of capitalist accumulation toward the concentration and centralization of capital, which necessarily leads to greater efficiency and higher productivity, there is a tendency of the average rate of profit to decline. Arguing against the view that the falling rate of profit is the result of increasing competition, Marx maintained that the rate of profit depends on the specific relationship between the rate of exploitation and the organic composition of capital. (In this sense, efficiency and productivity are not immediately related to profit.) For Marx, the tendency of the rate of profit to decline stems from the realization that the organic composition of capital increases more rapidly than the rate of exploitation. At any given time, therefore, so long as the organic composition of capital rises, the rate of profit must fall. In this way, there is a fundamental conflict between the expansion of production and the expansion of surplus value:

> The rate of profit falls, although the rate of surplus value remains the same or rises, because the proportion of variable capital to constant capital decreases with the development of the productive power of labor. The rate of profit thus falls, not because labor becomes less productive, but because it becomes more productive.[61]

The law of the tendency of the rate of profit to fall states that the total capital invested in production is divided between constant capital (*c*), capital advanced in the means of production, and variable capital (*v*), capital advanced in wages to the workers. The organic composition of capital reflects the application of technological progress to production and expresses the ratio between constant and variable capital (*c:v*). Technological progress, which increases productivity, causes the organic composition of capital to rise, that is, more capital is spent on the purchase for the means of production (*c*) than on the purchase of labor power (*v*), and thus a fall in the rate of profit. However, a decline in the average rate of profit does not mean that there is also a decline in the absolute mass of profit. On the contrary, a decline in the average rate of profit results in an increase in the absolute mass of profit due to the expansion of capitalist accumulation and capitalist production. The creation of a relative overpopulation of labor, for example, signifies that the capitalist can intensify the rate of exploitation, thus directly increasing the mass of profit.

Marx, however, noted five main "counteracting influences" to the law of the falling rate of profit, thus implying that this is indeed a tendential law. These are the following: (1) "increasing intensity of exploitation," which means an increase of constant capital as compared with variable capital, and thus a fall of the rate of profit; (2) "depression of wages below the value of labor power"; (3) "cheapening of elements of constant variable" (machines, raw materials, etc.,) through capital-savings innovations, which reduce the organic composition of capital; (4) "relative overpopulation" maintained through the growth of the industrial reserve army of labor, which slows down the growth of the average organic composition of capital; (5) "foreign trade," which cheapens the elements of both constant and variable capital, thus reducing the organic composition of capital and increasing the rate of surplus value.[62]

This notion of the tendency of the rate of profit to decline has significant implications for the way Marxian political economy understands the contradictions inherent in capitalist production and accumulation. First, the tendency of the rate of profit to fall signifies that capitalist accumulation cannot be, by its very nature, "stagnant." Capitalism must always reorganize itself and "promote its self-expansion to the highest limit."[63] But given the contradictory nature of capitalist accumulation, capitalism will always enter into systemic economic and social crises.

Capitalist crises are inherent in the nature of capital itself and arise from the tendency of the rate of profit to fall. This tendency "breeds overproduction, speculation, crises, and surplus-capital alongside surplus-population."[64] As such, the decline in the rate of profit is the result of the organic composition of capital to rise more rapidly than the rate of surplus value. It does not result from the failure to realize surplus value in the sphere of circulation. Underconsumptionism as the cause of crises was firmly rejected by Marx. The underconsumptionist thesis is simply incomparable with the basic postulate that capitalist contradictions derive from the operation of the law of value. For instance, it seems clear that by resorting to underconsumptionism as the cause of crises one would be led to believe that capitalist crises could be avoided by increases in wages that would increase in turn the purchasing power of the workers. This notion, however, is intrinsically absurd. Any increase in wages that would make a significant difference in the consuming power of the workers would begin to reduce the rate of profit. Yet it is precisely the falling rate of profit that constitutes the primary cause of crises. As Marx then pointed out,

> It is sheer tautology to say that crises are caused by the scarcity of effective consumption, or of effective consumers. The capitalist system does not know any other modes of consumption than effective ones, except that of *sub forma pauperis* or of the swindler. . . . But if one were to attempt to give this tautology the semblance of a profounder justification by saying that the working-class receives too small a portion of its own product and the evil would be remedied as soon as it receives a larger share of it and its wages increase in consequence, one could only remark that crises are always prepared by precisely a period in which wages rise generally and the working-class actually gets a larger share of that part of the annual product which is intended for consumption.[65]

At the heart of crises in capitalism is the exploitation of labor by capital. Capitalist crisis represents an overproduction of capital, that is, the overaccumulation of capital which can no longer be used to its full capacity. Crises of overproduction reflect the contradiction between socialized production and private appropriation, and the tendency of producers to produce commodities that "may not correspond to the market demand."[66] Consequently, overproduction provokes a decline in real wages and a rise in mass unemployment. However, overproduction crisis does not signify the permanent paralysis of capitalism. Capitalist accumulation is a dynamic process that can always reorganize itself on a higher scale. Thus, as one writer has noted, "if crisis reveals the inability of capital to overcome its barriers, it also shows itself to be the most powerful means for temporarily breaking through them."[67] The expansion of capitalism beyond the domestic market and into the world market is merely a reflection of the "dialectical process of the destruction and restructuring of capital."[68] It means that capitalism is leading itself into the monopolized stage of capitalism, and thus to crises, as Marx predicted, "on a higher scale, and finally to its violent overthrow."[69]

Marx's predictions about the overthrow of capitalism have not yet been borne out. No socialist revolution has taken place, as Marx had expected, in an advanced capitalist society. But this "fact" is hardly sufficient to declare Marx's analyses, or his vision, historically obsolete. For that matter, Marx never alluded to a specific time frame when discussing the overthrow of capitalism. Of course, it is also true that capitalism has shown greater resilience than what Marx seems at times to have suggested. Even so, when viewed from a dialectical and objective point of view, Marx's analyses and predictions about the evolution and development of capitalism are in fact quite sound. Marx disclosed with great rigor and accuracy the dynamics of the capitalist mode of production. Consider, for example, the following remarks from Wassily Leontief:

> The record is really impressive: increasing concentration of wealth, rapid elimination of small and medium-sized enterprise, incessant technological progress accompanied by the ever-growing importance of fixed capital, and, last but not least, the undiminishing amplitude of recurrent business cycles—an unsurpassed series of prognostications fulfilled, against which modern economic theory with all its refinements has little to show.[70]

There are other points that we should note with reference to the validity of Marx's politico-economic project. First, the "Marxian" *vision* has guided millions of people throughout the world. In this context the Russian and Chinese revolutions stand out as outstanding historical examples. The same applies to the struggle of many national liberation movements in the Third World. The working-class people in the advanced capitalist countries, on the other hand, are enjoying today certain basic social rights, thanks primarily to their historic, socialist-inspired struggle against capitalist exploitation. Second, in terms of an objective assessment of the "Marxian" vision, it is worth bearing in mind that Marxism has been employed as a political weapon by individuals and regimes seeking to establish authoritarian and absolutist political systems. Marxism cannot and should not be associated with such regimes. In fact, what happened in the latter part of 1989 in Eastern Europe is in many ways consistent with what Marx had always emphasized: oppression breeds revolt.

MARX ON IMPERIALISM

Marx's analysis of the capitalist mode of production makes no explicit reference to capitalist imperialism. Marx never developed a theory of imperialism. His comments on the subject matter are mostly journalistic in nature. Furthermore, it is difficult to deny that the multifaceted complexity of the late twentieth century is far greater than the stage of capitalism analyzed by Marx.

Even so, it would be a mistake to draw the conclusion from all this that Marx's analysis of the capitalist mode of production has no relevance for modern-day capitalism. Though it is true that Marx's analysis of the capitalist mode of production corresponds to the era of competitive capitalism, it is equally true that, in his theoretical exposition, "the notion of dynamic competition . . . leads directly to the theory of concentration and of the centralization of capital."[71] As a result, his theory has applicability under monopolistic conditions as well.

To understand imperialism without taking into serious consideration Marx's analysis of capitalism is impossible. For what Marx studied and analyzed in the *Das Kapital* was not only capitalism in a given social formation—for example, British capitalism, French capitalism, and so on—but the structural process, the dynamics, and the contradictions of the capitalist mode of production as a whole. Marx predicted not only the concentration and centralization of capital, but also clearly demonstrated that capitalism is an expansionist socio-economic system.

Marx's reflections on capitalist expansion suggest, as Albert Szymanski has correctly pointed out, "that there have been three historical phases in the relationship between the more advanced capitalist countries and the economically less-developed areas of the world: the stages of plunder, exploitation through trade and taxes, and investment in industry."[72] In both the first and second stages, where merchant capital dominates, exploitation of the underdeveloped countries of the world by the industrialized capitalist countries served to increase the material wealth in the former but without radically transforming the modes of production and the social relations of the latter (although trade and the export of goods disrupted in a fundamental way their social fabric). This point is well illustrated by Marx in his discussion of British rule in India:

> There have been in Asia, generally, from immemorial times, but three departments of Government: that of Finance, or the plunder of the interior; that of War, or the plunder of the exterior; and finally, the department of Public Works.
>
> Now, the British in East India accepted from their predecessors the departments of finance and of war, but they have neglected entirely that of public works. Hence the deterioration of an agriculture which is not capable of being conducted on the British principle of free competition, of *laissez-faire* and *laissez-aller*. But in Asiatic empires we are quite accustomed to see agriculture deteriorating under one government and reviving again under some other government. There the harvests correspond to good or bad governments, as they change in Europe with good or bad seasons. Thus the oppression and neglect of agriculture, bad as it is, could not be looked upon as the final blow dealt to Indian society by the British intruder, had it not been attended by a circumstance of quite different importance, a novelty in the annals of the whole Asiatic world. However changing the political aspect of India's past must appear, its social condi-

> tion has remained unaltered since its remotest antiquity, until the first decennium of the 19th century.[73]

However, during the third stage of capitalist expansion "the developed capitalist countries industrialize the less-developed countries, with industrial capital now flowing from the rich countries to the poor."[74] Through the establishment of the dominance of industrial capital over merchant capital, which compels the less-developed countries of the world to the adoption of capitalist production, capitalism is moving in the direction of the creation of a world capitalist economy. With the emergence of a world capitalist economy, the developed capitalist countries begin to invest capital abroad so that they can effectively promote industrialization in order to create the necessary conditions for the continued reproduction of capital. Correspondingly, the export of capital results in the radical transformation of the modes of production of less-developed countries and paves the way for their industrialization and eventual integration into the system of capitalist relations of production. Thus, in reference again to India, Marx observed:

> Till then the interests of the moneyocracy which had converted India into its landed estates, of the oligarchy who had conquered it by their armies, and of the millocracy who had inundated it with their fabrics, had gone hand in hand. But the more the industrial interest became dependent on the Indian market, the more it felt the necessity of creating fresh productive powers in India, after having ruined her native industry. You cannot continue to inundate a country with your manufactures, unless you enable it to give you some produce in return.[75]

More specifically:

> I know that the English millocracy intend to endow India with railways with the exclusive view of extracting at

> diminished expenses the cotton and other raw materials for their manufactures. But when you have once introduced machinery into the locomotion of a country, which possesses iron and coals, you are unable to withhold it from its fabrication. You cannot maintain a net of railways over an immense country without introducing all those industrial processes necessary to meet the immediate and current wants of railway locomotion, and out of which there must grow the application of machinery to those branches of industry not immediately connected with railways. The railway system will therefore become, in India, truly the forerunner of modern industry.[76]

The fundamental theme which runs through all of Marx's writings on capitalist expansion is that the logic of the accumulation of capital constantly propels capitalists to improve the instruments of production and to expand to foreign markets in search for cheap raw materials and more profitable opportunities. In Marx and Engels's words:

> The bourgeoisie cannot exist without constantly revolutionizing the instruments of production, and thereby the relations of production, and with them the whole relations of society.
>
> The need of a constantly expanding market for its products chases the bourgeoisie over the whole surface of the globe. It must nestle everywhere, settle everywhere, establish connections everywhere.[77]

Expansion into foreign markets is indeed of special importance to capitalism. Yet it is significant to note that foreign markets are not necessary conditions for the appearance of capitalism. The expansion of foreign markets is a result of the tendency of the rate of profit to fall. It is the realization of the need for a higher rate of profit that compels capitalists to invest abroad. At the same time, the mere participation of the pre-capitalistic countries in the world market does not mean that these societies have become capitalistic. In fact, it is clear from Marx's observations about capitalist expansion that he did not consider the less-developed countries of the world as being capitalist. He theorized, however, that in due time capitalism would destroy pre-capitalist economies. In any case, for Marx, as Anthony Brewer correctly states, there is no conception of capitalism on the basis of "a centre-periphery division on a world scale. . . . "[78]

In addition, there can be no doubt that Marx considered capitalist expansion to be a "progressive" rather than a "regressive" movement. It is worth quoting Marx and Engels here at some length:

> The bourgeoisie, by the rapid improvement of all instruments of production, by the immensely facilitated means of communication, draws all, even the most barbarian, nations into civilization. The cheap prices of its commodities are the heavy artillery with which it batters down all Chinese walls, with which it forces the barbarians' intensely obstinate hatred of foreigners to capitulate. It compels all nations, on pain of extinction, to adopt the bourgeois mode of production; it compels them to introduce what it calls civilization into their midst, i.e., to become bourgeois themselves. In one word, it creates a world after its own image.
>
> The bourgeoisie has subjected the country to the rule of the towns. It has created enormous cities, has greatly increased the urban population as compared with the rural, and has thus rescued a considerable part of the population from the idiocy of rural life. Just as it has made the country dependent on the towns, so it has made barbarian and semi-barbarian countries dependent on the civilized ones, nations of peasants on nations of bourgeois, the East on the West.[79]

Marx was hardly ignorant or insensitive to the evils associated with the expansion of capitalism. His seemingly enthusiastic approval of the spread of capitalism stemmed from his firm belief that the inevitable result in the operation of industrial capitalist expansion is none other than the establishment of the necessary historical conditions for the materialization and eventual realization of a socialist world order:

> The bourgeois period of history has to create the material basis of the new world—on the one hand the universal intercourse founded upon the mutual dependence of mankind, and the means of that intercourse; on the other hand the development of the productive forces of man and the transformation of material production into a scientific domination of natural agencies. Bourgeois industry and commerce create these material conditions of a new world in the same way as geological revolutions have created the surface of the earth. When a great social revolution shall have mastered the results of the bourgeois epoch, the market of the world and the modern powers of production, and subjected them to the common control of the most advanced peoples, then only will human progress cease to resemble that hideous pagan idol, who would not drink the nectar but from the skull of the slain.[80]

Indeed, as we have noted earlier, for Marx, capitalism contains an inherent tendency toward the determination of those conditions and possibilities which are essential for the emancipation of labor. This assumption is based as much on Marx's dialectical method as in his specific empirical studies. Marx grasped more clearly than anyone of his contemporaries the economic fact that capitalism was leading society toward the socialization of production, or more fundamentally, that the logic of capitalist development was advancing society from the realm of necessity to the realm of freedom. Hence as Andrew Linklater has written:

> Capitalism could be condemned in Marx's view for . . . creating seemingly unprecedented opportunities for the expression of the full range of human powers while reducing labor

> to the performance of purely repetitive and mechanical tasks; and for bringing about an extraordinary increase in the level of social power over nature while placing individuals at the mercy of international market forces which they were powerless to control.[81]

It should be pointed out here that Marx did not exclude the possibility of the emergence of socialism prior to the spread of capitalism. During the 1880s Marx expressed the view that it might be conceivable for Russia to make the transition to socialism without going first through the stage of capitalism.[82] But as many commentators have pointed out, there is no good reason to take this particular view by Marx very seriously.[83] Furthermore, there is no evidence whatsoever to suggest that Marx deviated in any possible theoretical way from the centrality of his proposition, which is that the dynamics and contradictions of capitalism were paving the way for a socialist world. Paradoxically, the neo-Marxists, as we shall see later, have employed a theoretical analysis which treats the phenomenon of imperialism from a conceptual angle which obscures or even rejects Marx's emphasis on the historic mission of capitalism. However, to reject the historic mission of capitalism means to reject, in the final analysis, the goal and aspiration of Marxism itself: "Workers of the World Unite."

SUMMARY AND CONCLUSION

This chapter had dealt with the essential methodological and theoretical foundations of Marxian political economy. The Marxian method of analysis is concerned with the laws of social development and the dynamics of social change. In this endeavor, the socio-economic system of capitalism constitutes the primary focus of Marxian social inquiry. Thus, in considering the method and principles of Marxian political economy, we encounter a number of core claims: (1) social change is an objective development governed by economic laws, in the course of which the class struggle functions as a catalyst in the transition from one social order to another; (2) the "laws of motion" of the capitalist mode of production are (a) the concentration and centralization of capital; (b) the growth in the organic composition of capital; (c) the tendency of the average rate of profit to fall; and (d) the objective socialization of production; (3) crises of overproduction represent the inner contradictions of the capitalist system; and, (4) that capitalism is a progressive force in that it prepares the foundation for the emergence of a socialist order.

No serious Marxist would think of suggesting that Marx's politico-economic project is sufficient for understanding and explaining contemporary social reality. But we do think that Marx's work is necessary for such an undertaking.[84] The basic principles of historical materialism and Marxian political economy are as valid today as ever. This view will guide our analysis in the forthcoming chapters.

NOTES

1. Some clarifications are necessary with regard to the interpretation of Marxian political economy presented here. First, the recognition of Marx's politico-economic project as scientific does not in any way imply uncritical acceptance of the views and claims registered in it by Marx. Indeed, any attempt to consider Marx's work and system of thought in general in a dogmatic fashion must be entirely rejected. Dogmatism violates the very spirit of Marx's understanding of science as well as that of reality itself. The designation of Marx's political economy as scientific in nature and content is formed on the basis of its methodological and theoretical approach which regarded the endeavor to come to terms with the inner logic of reality as the distinctive feature of any scientific enquiry. Within this context, Marxian political economy is scientific by virtue of the fact that it makes a sharp distinction between appearance and essence. For as Marx put it, "all science would be superfluous if the outward appearance and the essence of things directly coincided." See Karl Marx, *Capital*, vol. 3 (New York: International Publishers, 1967), 817. In the second place, by referring to Marxian political economy as a revolutionary science, we simply mean that Marx's politico-economic project is not merely an intellectual achievement, but also a practical guide to the problems facing the working-class people in capitalist society. Insofar as the Marxian political economy demonstrates that capital-

ism is an anarchic and contradictory system of social organization, which thrives on exploitation and oppression, it becomes a revolutionary force of overpowering ability by giving meaning and substance to the conscious need of the working class to construct a socialist society.

2. See Karl Marx, *The Poverty of Philosophy*, in *Collected Works*, vol. 6 (New York: International Publishers, 1976), pp. 162, 166; quoted in Louis Althusser and Etienne Balibar, *Reading Capital* (London: Verso, 1979), 92.

3. See Karl Marx, *Capital*, vol. 1 (New York: International Publishers, 1967), p. 14; quoted in Roger Garaudy, *Karl Marx: The Evolution of His Thought* (Westport, Conn: Greenwood Press, 1976), p. 122.

4. Karl Marx, *Capital*, vol. 1, p. 171.

5. For an interesting and challenging discussion of Marx's epistemology and methodological approach, see Alfred Schmidt, *History and Structure: An Essay on Hegelian-Marxist and Structuralist Theories of History* (Cambridge, MA: The MIT Press, 1983), especially pp. 29–134.

6. Thus, Eric Hobsbawm summarizes the significance of Marx's method of analysis, especially for historians, as follows:

> Marx remains the essential base of any adequate study of history, because—so far—he alone has attempted to formulate a methodological approach to history as a whole, and to envisage and explain the entire process of human evolution. In this respect he is superior to Max Weber, his only real rival as a theoretical influence on historians, and in many respects an important supplement and corrective. A history based on Marx is conceivable without Weberian additions, but Weberian history is inconceivable except insofar as it takes Marx, or at least the Marxist Fragestellung, as its starting point.

Eric Hobsbawm, "Marx and History," *New Left Review*, no. 143 (January-February 1984): 48.

7. Karl Marx and Friedrich Engels, *The German Ideology, Collected Works*, vol. 5 (New York: International Publishers, 1976), p. 28.

8. Nicos Poulantzas, *Political Power and Social Classes* (London: New Left Books, 1973), p. 11.

9. Karl Marx, *A Contribution to the Critique of Political Economy* (New York: International Publishers, 1970), pp. 20–21.

10. Aware of the problems associated with Marx's formulation of historical materialism in the Preface to *A Contribution of the Critique of Political Economy*, Alex Callinicos presents instead a "summary of historical materialism," as developed by Marx in the third volume of the *Das Kapital*. It reads as follows:

> The specific economic form, in which unpaid surplus-labor is pumped out of direct producers, determines the relationship of rulers and ruled,

> as it grows directly out of production itself and , in turn, reacts upon it as a determining element. Upon this, however, is founded the formation of the economic community which grows out of the production relations themselves, thereby simultaneously its specific political form. It is always the direct relationship of the owners of the conditions of production to the direct producers—a relationship always naturally corresponding to a definite stage in the development of the methods of labor and thereby its social productivity—which reveals the innermost secret, the hidden basis of the entire social structure, and with it the political form of the relation of sovereignty and dependence, in short, the corresponding specific form of the state.

The merit of this formulation is that the productive forces, as Callinicos notes, constitute themselves a social activity, thus giving greater strength to the argument that historical materialism is not a technologically deterministic conception of history. See Alex Callinicos, *Making History* (Ithaca, NY: Cornell University Press, 1988), pp. 41–64.

11. Isaiah Berlin, *Karl Marx: His Life and Environment* (New York: Oxford University Press, 1963), p. 122.

12. As is well known, the formulation of an economistic and evolutionist interpretation of historical materialism was originally developed by the theoreticians of the Second International—for example, Kautsky and Plekhanov and the like—and eventually codified into a dogma by Stalin's diamat. For the reconstruction of historical materialism as a technologically deterministic conception of history see, in particular, G. A. Cohen, *Karl Marx's Theory of History: A Defense* (Oxford: Clarendon Press, 1978); John McMurtry, *The Structure of Marx's World-View* (Princeton, NJ: Princeton University Press, 1978); William H. Shaw, *Marx's Theory of History* (Stanford, CA: Stanford University Press, 1978).

13. Karl Marx, *A Contribution to the Critique of Political Economy*, p. 206.

14. Ibid., p. 206.

15. Karl Marx and Friedrich Engels, *The German Ideology*, p. 53.

16. Kenneth Neill Cameron, *Marxism: The Science of Society* (South Hadley, MA: Bergin & Garvey Publishers, 1985), p. 19.

17. Friedrich Engels to Conrad Schmidt, in Karl Marx and Friedrich Engels *Selected Correspondence, 1846–1895*, trans. Dora Torr (Westport, CT: Greenwood Press, 1975), p. 473.

18. Derek Sayer, *Marx's Method: Ideology, Science and Critique in Capital* (Hassocks, England: Harvester Press, 1979), p. 94; quoted in Gregor McLennan, *Marxism and the Methodologies of History* (London: New Left Books, 1981), p. 42.

19. See Derek Sayer, *The Violence of Abstraction: The Analytic Foundations of Historical Materialism* (New York: Basil Blackwell, 1987), p. 13.

20. G. A. Cohen, *Karl Marx's Theory of History: A Defense*, p. 32.

21. See, for example, ibid., p. 113.

22. Karl Marx and Friedrich Engels, *The German Ideology*, p. 43.

23. The "mode of production" is conceived by Marx in the *Das Kapital* as a set of relationships referring to the specific interaction between the productive forces and the social relations of production. See Karl Marx, *Capital*, vol. 1, p. 510. David Harvey, however, has correctly pointed out that Marx uses the term "mode of production" in at least two different ways besides the one suggested above. He notes, for example, that in some instances Marx uses the term to refer to "the actual methods and techniques used in the production of a particular kind of use value." And, sometimes, "particularly in his preparatory writings such as the *Grundrisse*," Marx uses the term to refer "to the whole gamut of production, exchange, distribution and consumption relations as well as to the institutional, juridical and administrative arrangements, political organization and state apparatus, ideology and characteristic forms of social (class) reproduction." See David Harvey, *The Limits to Capital* (Chicago: The University of Chicago Press, 1982), p. 25.

24. The primitive-communal system represents the only type of society that was not structured on the basis of classes. The means of production under so-called primitive communism were communally owned.

25. Nikolai Bukharin, *Historical Materialism: A System of Sociology* (Ann Arbor: The University of Michigan Press, 1976), p. 282.

26. Karl Marx and Friedrich Engels, *Manifesto of the Communist Party, Collected Works*, vol. 6 (New York: International Publishers, 1976), p. 489.

27. Karl Marx, *Capital*, vol. 1, p. 763.

28. See Karl Marx and Friedrich Engels, *Manifesto of the Communist Party*, p. 506.

29. Although Marx never developed a systematic theory of the state, he still regarded it to be an important theme for discussion (which he actually planned to undertake immediately upon the completion of his studies of capitalism) and made frequent reference to the role and function of the state throughout his political and historical writings. As things stand, however, the state occupies a rather dubious position in Marx's work. For example, in many instances Marx employs the notion of the state in terms of an instrument used by the "ruling class" to secure its interests in capitalist society. See, in particular, Marx and Engels, *Manifesto of the Communist Party*, in *Collected Works*, vol. 6, p. 486; and *The German Ideology*, in *Collected Works*, vol. 5, p. 90. At times, on the other hand, Marx presents a view of the state as being relatively autonomous from the immediate interests of the most dominant economic classes

and, in general, treats the state as a factor of cohesion in the social formation. See Karl Marx, *The Eighteenth Brumaire of Louis Bonaparte*, in *Selected Works* in one volume (New York: International Publishers, 1968), pp. 168–80. For an extended version of the idea that one encounters in Marx two different, although not necessarily unrelated, views of the state, see Ralph Miliband, "Marx and the State," *Socialist Register* (London: Merlin Press, 1965). For a systematic treatment of the state possessing "relative" autonomy, see Nicos Poulantzas, *Political Power and Social Classes*, pp. 258–62. Finally, for a truly outstanding work on various Marxist theories of the state, see Bob Jessop, *The Capitalist State: Marxist Theories and Methods* (New York: New York University Press, 1982).

30. Karl Marx, *The Eighteenth Brumaire of Louis Bonaparte*, p. 97.

31. Karl Marx and Friedrich Engels, *Manifesto of the Communist Party*, p. 482.

32. For a further discussion on this point, see Jorge Larrain, *A Reconstruction of Historical Materialism* (London: Allen & Unwin, 1986), pp. 84–91.

33. There are many useful works that have explored Marx's concept of the Asiatic mode of production. See, for example, Anne M. Bailey and Josep R. Llobera, eds., *The Asiatic Mode of Production: Science and Politics* (London: Routledge and Kegan Paul, 1981); Lawrence Krader, *The Asiatic Mode of Production: Sources, Development, and Critique in the Writings of Karl Marx* (Assen, The Netherlands: Van Gorcum, 1975); Brendan O'Leary, *The Asiatic Mode of Production: Oriental Despotism, Historical Materialism, and Indian History* (New York: Basil Blackwell, 1989); and Marian Sawer, *Marxism and the Question of the Asiatic Mode of Production* (The Hague: Martinus Nijhoff, 1977).

34. This is the case, for example, with Louis Althusser. See Louis Althusser and Etienne Balibar, *Reading Capital*.

35. Marx to the editor of the Otyecestvenniye Zapisky, *Selected Correspondence, 1846–1895*, pp. 353–54.

36. V. I. Lenin, "On the So-Called Market Question," in *Collected Works*, vol. 1 (Moscow: Progress Publishers, 1972), p. 93.

37. Karl Marx, *Capital*, vol. 1, p. 35.

38. Ibid., p. 39.

39. Ibid., p. 80.

40. Ibid., p. 61.

41. For a unique and penetrating study on the Marxian theory of value, see John Weeks, *Capital and Exploitation* (Princeton, NJ: Princeton University Press, 1981), pp. 11–62.

42. This point is discussed with brilliance in Lucio Colletti, *From Rousseau to Lenin* (New York: Monthly Review Press, 1974), pp. 82–93.

43. One of the best discussions on the concept of abstract labor is Simon Mohun, "Abstract Labor and Its Value-Form," *Science and Society*, vol. 48, no. 4 (Winter 1984–85): 388–406.
44. Bade Onimode, *An Introduction to Marxist Political Economy* (London: Zed Books, 1985), p. 71.
45. Karl Marx, *Capital*, vol. 1, p. 58.
46. Ibid., p. 150.
47. Ibid., p. 164.
48. Ibid., pp. 165–66.
49. Ibid., p. 167.
50. Ibid., p. 167
51. Ibid., p. 169.
52. Ibid., p. 551.
53. Ibid., p. 539.
54. See Meghnad Desai, *Marxian Economic Theory* (London: Gray-Mills Publishing, 1974), p. 23.
55. Karl Marx, *Capital*, vol. 3, pp. 814–15.
56. Karl Marx, *Capital*, vol. 1, p. 644.
57. This particular point is brilliantly discussed by John Weeks, *Capital and Exploitation*, pp. 158–66.
58. Karl Marx, *Grundrisse*, translated with a foreword by Martin Nicolaus (New York: Vintage Books, 1973), p. 414.
59. Karl Marx, *Capital*, vol. 1, p. 763.
60. Karl Marx, *Grundrisse*, p. 414.
61. Karl Marx, *Theories of Surplus Value*, vol. 2 (London: Lawrence and Wishart, 1969), p. 439.
62. See Karl Marx, *Capital*, vol. 3, pp. 232–40.
63. Ibid., p. 249.
64. Ibid., p. 242.
65. Karl Marx, *Capital*, vol. 2, pp. 410–11; quoted in John Weeks, "The Sphere of Production and the Analysis of Crisis in Capitalism," *Science and Society*, vol. 41, no. 3 (Fall 1977): 285.
66. V. I. Lenin, "The Lessons of the Crisis," in *Collected Works*, vol. 5 (Moscow: Progress Publishers, 1972), p. 90.
67. Raymond Lotta with Frank Shannon, *America in Decline*, vol. 1 (Chicago: Banner Press, 1984), pp. 65–66.
68. Ibid., p. 56.
69. Karl Marx, *Grundrisse*, pp. 750; quoted in Raymond Lotta, *America in Decline*, p. 70.
70. Quoted in Karl Kühne, *Economics and Marxism, Volume I: The Renaissance of the Marxian System* (New York: St. Martin's Press, 1979), p. 40.
71. Ibid., p. 267.

72. Albert Szymanski, *The Logic of Imperialism* (New York: Praeger Publishers, 1981), p. 23.

73. Karl Marx, "The British Rule in India," in Karl Marx and Friedrich Engels, *On Colonialism* (New York: International Publishers, 1972), pp. 37–38.

74. Albert Szymanski, *The Logic of Imperialism*, p. 23.

75. Karl Marx, "The East India Company—Its History and Results," in Karl Marx and Friedrich Engels, *On Colonialism*, p. 52.

76. Karl Marx, "The Future Results of the British Rule in India," in Karl Marx and Friedrich Engels, *On Colonialism*, pp. 84–85.

77. Karl Marx and Friedrich Engels, *Manifesto of the Communist Party*, p. 489.

78. Anthony Brewer, *Marxist Theories of Imperialism: A Critical Survey* (London: Routledge and Kegan Paul, 1980), p. 44.

79. Karl Marx and Friedrich Engels, *Manifesto of the Communist Party*, p. 488.

80. Karl Marx, "The Future Results of the British Rule in India," p. 87.

81. See Andrew Linklater, *Beyond Realism and Marxism: Critical Theory and International Relations* (New York: St. Martin's Press, 1990), p. 43.

82. This whole issue is addressed in a detailed, although misconceived, I believe, fashion in Teodor Shanin, ed., *Late Marx and the Russian Road* (London: Routledge and Kegan Paul, 1983).

83. This claim, for example, is made by M. C. Howard and J. E. King, *A History of Marxian Economics, Volume 1, 1883–1929* (Princeton: Princeton University Press, 1989), pp. 137–40.

84. In a recent and very provocative work, Tryphon Kostopoulos, *Beyond Capitalism Toward Nomocracy* (New York: Praeger Publishers, 1986) develops the argument that Marxism as a system of thought is no longer valid because capitalism itself has become historically obsolete. Such a claim, of course, is firmly rejected in our study. Nonetheless, it is interesting to note that the author rejects Marxism not because it is impotent in explaining capitalist reality, but rather because the latter itself has lost its historical essence.

2

Classical Marxist Theories of Imperialism

At the end of the nineteenth century and beginning of the twentieth, the tendency toward the concentration and centralization of capital (as Marx had predicted) emerged as the greatest economic change in the whole course of development of the capitalist economic system. The stages of this process were initiated by the revolutionization of the productive forces of capitalism and the subsequent application of new methods and techniques in capitalist industry. With improved planning and organization of production, a small number of large economic enterprises gained the upper hand and, as a rule, came to dominate over the major areas of capitalist life. The underlying result of this was the transformation of competitive capitalism into monopoly capitalism, in which the spread abroad for more profitable markets was the essential feature. This is where the phenomenon of capitalist imperialism first appears.

These changes in the development of capitalism became the central concern of the early Marxist theoreticians. A number of significant studies were produced at that time, which attempted to develop a theoretical framework for explaining the essence and the implications of imperialism. Thus the beginnings of Marxist theories of imperialism date back to the very early part of the twentieth century.

The present chapter reviews the theories of Hobson, Hilferding, Luxemburg, Bukharin, and Lenin, and highlights their fundamental differences and similarities. The theories of these thinkers will be discussed in the order in which they were written rather than published.

HOBSON

John Atkinson Hobson, an Englishman, and a member of the British Liberal Party, was one of the first writers to formulate a theory of imperialism.[1] A staunch adherent of the social-liberal tradition, Hobson's study constructed a theory of imperialism which sharply criticized England's aggressive foreign policy particularly because of its adverse effects on the economic and political structures of British capitalist society. In fact, Hobson's theoretical construction of imperialism can only be understood within the context of his social-liberal political or ideological orientations. Then why, one might ask, include Hobson in a study devoted to Marxist theories of imperialism? Because, some Marxists would say, while Hobson's views are certainly more in order with the social-liberal rather than the Marxist tradition, they constitute the base or the "source" of Lenin's theoretical procedures.[2]

How very wrong. It is true of course that Hobson's analysis influenced Lenin's theory of imperialism. But it is, among other things, a myth that Lenin's thinking proceeded on the basis of the theoretical construction developed by Hobson.[3] Consequently we include Hobson in this study to dispel this myth.

The distinctive theoretical premise upon which Hobson's analysis of imperialism rests is the notion that capitalism has the inherent ability to serve society in a rational and humane way. Or, to rephrase this, competitive capitalism and free trade represent a rational form of economic organization which can serve the interests of a given country and the world as a whole. In this sense, Hobson is very much in the tradition of the political economy of Adam Smith.[4] At the same time he distinguished himself from the philosophy of laissez-faire capitalism by advocating state action to promote progress, reform, and peace.

Hobson's study and critique of imperialism reflects the representation of his political or ideological convictions. It is marked by his unshaking belief that imperialism violates liberal values and practices. For example, it challenges imperialism on the ground that it contributes to and participates in the formation of protectionism. Holding firm to the idea that the acquisition of colonies was not necessary for trade to follow, Hobson argued that imperialism not only did not improve trade relations with other countries of the world but coincided with the suppression of free trade. In addition, he argued that imperialism and its methods are antithetical to the methods and principles of liberal representative institutions. That is, Hobson believed that imperialism could only survive by endeavouring to foster autocratic forms of government abroad. He feared, moreover, that the liberal democratic nations, such as England and the United States, would not be able to escape from the effects of the forms and practices of political domination unleashed by imperialism in the less-developed countries of the world. Thus, he wrote as follows: "It is, indeed, a nemesis of Imperialism that the arts and crafts of tyranny, acquired and exercised in our unfree Empire, should be turned against our liberties at home."[5]

Despite a common view to the contrary, Hobson's study mystified the problem concerning the transition of competitive capitalism to monopoly capitalism—and hence the question of imperialism. To begin with there is nothing in Hobson's analysis to suggest that he understood even the most basic economic law of capitalism: namely, to quote Lenin, that "free competition gives rise to the concentration of production, which, in turn, at a certain stage of development, leads to monopoly."[6] It is true, of course, that he recognized that the character of the economic forces at work in the industrial capitalist countries of his time was undergoing fundamental changes. "The growing cosmopolitanism of capital," he wrote, "has been the greatest economic change of recent generations."[7] He was also aware of the fact that certain classes in particular benefited from the increasing tendencies toward the export of capital to the less-developed regions of the world. But little or no attempt was made by him to explain these changes in the context of the objective determination of the logic of the capitalist system itself. Hence despite his observations about capitalism's tendencies toward overproduction and the generation of excessive capital, he disposed of these contradictions with relative ease by criticizing business and state policy for failing to raise the consuming power of the masses. He wrote:

> It is admitted by all business men that the growth of the powers of production in their country exceeds the growth in consumption, that more goods can be produced than can be sold at a profit, and that more capital exists than can find remunerative investment.
>
> It is this economic condition of affairs that forms the taproot of Imperialism. If the consuming public in this country raised its standard of consumption to keep pace with every rise of productive powers, there could be no excess of goods or capital clamorous to use Imperialism in order to fill markets: foreign trade would indeed exist, but there would be no difficulty in exchanging a small surplus of our manufactures for the food and raw material we annually absorbed, and all the savings that we made could find employment, if we chose, in home industries.[8]

Hobson endorsed the view that imperialism was organically independent from capitalism. He thought that imperialism was a harmful social policy, reflecting the interests of big business, and that it had no place in a modern, liberal-capitalist society. With this as his clue, he proceeded to demonstrate that imperialism is located in the specific relationship between political structures, public opinion, and so-called "moneylending classes dressed as Imperialists and patriots."[9] Hobson doubtless did not believe that in order for imperialism to be effectively suppressed, capitalist economic relations had to be abolished. On the contrary, Hobson's analysis sought to convince capitalists that they had more to gain by investing at home rather than abroad.

Hobson's theory of imperialism has been accurately described as a "socio-psychological explanation of jingoism."[10] Without an understanding of the dynamics of capitalism, Hobson ended up reducing "the economic taproot of imperialism" into a political and social policy invented and directed by the members of certain classes in capitalist society. This is the foundation of his conception of imperialism. Thus, he wrote:

> It was this sudden demand for foreign markets for manufactures and for investments which was avowedly responsible for the adoption of Imperialism as a political policy and practice by the Republican party to which the great industrial and financial chiefs belonged, and which belonged to them. The adventurous enthusiasm of President Theodore Roosevelt and his "manifest destiny" and "mission of civilization" party must not deceive us. It was Messrs. Rockefeller, Pierpont Morgan, and their associates who needed Imperialism and who fastened it upon the shoulders of the great Republic of the West. They needed Imperialism because they desired to use the public resources of their country to find profitable employment for their capital which otherwise would be superfluous.[11]

In constructing his theory, Hobson also made a distinction between imperialism and colonialism. While he defined "imperialism" as essentially an aggressive foreign policy undertaken by the state on behalf of the economic interests of certain classes, he reserved the term "colonialism" to denote national self-expression and a movement of "peaceful" territorial expansion. Thus, he wrote that "colonialism, in its best sense, is a natural overflow of nationality; its test is the power of colonists to transplant the civilization they represent to the new natural and social environment in which they find themselves."[12]

According to this definition, colonialism may be regarded as the positive expression of nationalism oriented toward the realization of an interdependent world. Thus Hobson spoke at one and the same time against imperialism but in support of colonialism. Strongly influenced by the ideology of Eurocentrism and racism, Hobson felt that the progress of mankind dependent on a constant struggle between the "civilized" nations and what he called the "lower races."[13] Accordingly, he perceived European nationalism as "a plain highway to internationalism,"[14] whose goal and objective was to secure the superiority of the Western nations and culture and therefore guarantee the proper selection of those nations that would generate the tendencies toward progress and prosperity. "Effective internationalism," he wrote,

> is the only sound basis of competition and rational selection among nations. In the cruder form of the human struggle, accident, or numbers, or some primitive form of cunning, may secure the success of a people whose "social efficiency" is of a low order, impermanent and unproductive, while it stamps out or checks the growth of a people whose latent powers of achievement and capacities of progress are far superior. Only in proportion as racial or national selection is rationally guided and determined does the world gain security against such wastes and such calamities.[15]

Now we have come to the crux of the matter. For Hobson, nationalism can take one of two forms: internationalism or imperialism. Internationalism, resting on the base of free trade expansionism and colonialism, represents a progressive force by registering the logic of Western civilization on the less-developed countries of the world. Imperialism, on the other hand, reflects "an artificial stimulation of nationalism,"[16] and constitutes a regressive force because it hinders the spread of internationalism. In the first place, imperialism gives rise to strong movements abroad against the expansion of European nations by introducing brutal and autocratic forms of government. Moreover, imperialism, noted Hobson, develops alongside inter-imperialist rivalries. It thus becomes a necessity that in the process of imperialist competition for foreign markets militarism and war should assume dominant importance. In the context of such conditions, the Western nations would begin to degenerate to the point of being no longer able to spread the spirit of progress and civilization throughout the world. Indeed, Hobson left no doubt about what he thought were the effects of imperialism. He wrote: "Imperialism—whether it consists in a further policy of expansion or in the rigorous maintenance of all those vast tropical lands which have been earmarked as British spheres of influence—implies militarism now and ruinous wars in the future."[17]

To be sure, it was above all else Hobson's penetrating insights of the effects of imperialism that drew Lenin's attention. It was a common practice for Lenin to use bourgeois findings to support his own claims. But Lenin, as we shall see shortly, rejected wholeheartedly Hobson's theoretical perspective. As a result, it makes absolutely no sense at all to speak of a "Hobson-Lenin" thesis.

HILFERDING

Marx's theory of the development of capitalism, albeit uncomplete and somewhat fragmentary, anticipated the concentration and centralization of capital and the general tendency toward the formation of monopolies. Hobson, as we already saw, recognized but failed to provide a scientific treatment of the nature of those processes. His theory of imperialism distorted the objective determination of the logic of the capitalist system by defining the forces of monopoly capital in terms of the conscious expression of a social policy specific to certain class interests.

Rudolf Hilferding, a theorist associated with the Austro-Marxist school, was the first Marxist to attempt a theoretical formulation "of the economic characteristics of the latest phase of capitalist development."[18] Writing during the first decade of the twentieth century, Hilferding recognized the need to further develop Marx's analysis of capitalism. Within this context, he devoted special attention to the processes of the concentration and centralization of capital, and outlined a theory of imperialism as a necessary development in the evolution of capitalism. In the course of this process he also made it clear that systematic investigation on the role of money and credit, the expansion of capitalist enterprises and their conversion into corporations, and the cause of crises was of the utmost importance for the further development of Marxian political economy.

Hilferding shared with Marx the notion that the centralization and concentration of capital reflected the necessity of the growth of capitalism which enabled a small number of large capitalist enterprises to absorb smaller ones. Yet he went further than Marx on this by undertaking a thorough analysis of the modern corporation. He demonstrated that the rise of the industrial corporation reflects an objective "change in the function of the industrial capitalist."[19] The industrial corporation, or the joint-stock company, allows anyone in possession of money to become a money capitalist. In effect, what Hilferding was observing was the phenomenon of the separation of ownership of capital from control in the joint-stock company. According to him, this process not only accelerated the concentration of capital but provided the joint-stock company with the ability to expand far more rapidly than the individually owned enterprise, thereby leading to the centralization of capital as well.

For Hilferding, however, it was the emergence of financial institutions and banks, in particular, that truly intensified the processes toward concentration. He stressed that in the mature stage of capitalism, banks, which were quite necessary to the growth of industry, had become fully dominant and directly controlled the economic life of the system. Through its vast resources of liquid capital, banks were able to obtain control of major trusts in industry, since the latter needed idle capital in order to increase and expand the production process. Viewed from this perspective, industrial capital was inextricably intertwined with banking capital and wholly dependent on money capital. Hilferding formulated his conception of the relationship between banks and industrial capital in the latest stage of capitalist development in the following way:

> In this relationship the bank is the more powerful party. The bank always disposes over capital in its liquid, readily available, form: money capital. The enterprise, on the other hand, has to depend upon reconverting commodities into money. Should the circulation process come to a halt, or prices fall, the enterprise will require additional capital which can only be obtained in the form of credit. Under a developed credit system, an enterprise maintains its own capital at a minimum; any sudden need for additional liquid funds involves obtaining credit, and failure to do so may lead to bankruptcy. It is the bank's control of money capital which gives it a dominant position in its dealings with enterprises whose capital is tied up in production or in commodities.[20]

The merging process between industrial and banking capital gives rise to a new form of capital: finance capital. Accordingly, Hilferding defined finance capital as "capital at the disposition of the banks which is used by the industrialists."[21] Moreover, the establishment of an intimate relationship between banking capital and industrial capital results in an increased tendency toward the export of capital. The concentration of capital, which leads to monopolization, encourages the export of capital by virtue of the fact that the overaccumulation of capital, which is in itself connected with the new technological changes in the production process, can no longer find profitable investment opportunities at home. Hilferding presents a number of factors that accelerate the process of the export of capital.[22] Nevertheless, "the precondition for the export of capital," he wrote,

> is the variation in rates of profit, and the export of capital is the means of equalizing national rates of profit. The level of profit depends upon the organic composition of capital, that is to say, upon the degree of capitalist development. The

> more advanced it is the lower will be the rate of profit. . . . So far as the rate of interest is concerned it is much higher in underdeveloped capitalist countries, which lack extensive credit and banking facilities, than in advanced capitalist countries. Furthermore, interest in such countries still includes for the most part an element of wages or entrepreneurial profit. The high rate of interest is a direct inducement to the export of loan capital. Entrepreneurial profit is also higher because labor power is exceptionally cheap, and what it lacks in quality is made up by unusually long hours of work. In addition, since ground rent is very low or purely nominal . . . costs of production are low. Finally, profits are swelled by special privileges and monopolies.[23]

For Hilferding, the era of finance capital signifies the transition into the monopoly stage of capitalism—and hence the appearance of imperialism. The outcome of this process is intense economic competition at the international level, militarism, and war. Hilferding argued that under the influence of monopolistic combinations, the state is subordinated to the interests of finance capital and plays a leading role in the international arena by assisting and accommodating its particular needs through "the pursuit of an imperialist policy."[24] Moreover, he maintained that while international agreements and the formation of international cartels and trusts could reduce inter-imperialist rivalries, the antagonisms between national monopolistic combinations were so great that there was no prospect for the formation or realization of an "ultra-imperialist" model.

Finally, Hilferding argued that imperialism would help to industrialize the less-developed world but also create the conditions for the emergence of liberation movements seeking to overthrow the yoke of imperialism. He wrote:

> In the newly-opened countries themselves . . . the introduction of capitalism intensifies contradictions and arouses

> growing resistance to the invaders among the people, whose national consciousness has been awakened, which can easily take the form of policies inimical to foreign capital. The old social relations are completely revolutionized, the age-old bondage to the soil of the "nations without a history" is disrupted and they are swept into the capitalist maelstrom. Capitalism itself gradually provides the subjected people with the ways and means for their own liberation. They adopt as their own the ideal that was once the highest aspiration of the European nations; namely, the formation of a unified national state as an instrument of economic and cultural freedom. This independence movement threatens European capital precisely in its most valuable and promising areas of exploitation, and to an increasing extent it can only maintain its domination by continually expanding its means of coercion.[25]

Hilferding's *Finance Capital* is without a doubt an important contribution to Marxian political economy. His analysis, however, of the role of banks and the actual meaning of the term "finance capital" has received substantial criticism. Paul Sweezy, for example, has argued that "Hilferding mistakes a transitional phase of capitalist development for a lasting trend."[26] For Sweezy, the dependence of industrial capital on banking capital is not a permanent state of affairs. According to him, at some point in their development "the large monopolistic corporations find themselves . . . in possession of internal sources of funds," and break "their dependence on bankers."[27] Lenin, on the other hand, observed that Hilferding's definition of finance capital "is incomplete insofar as it is silent on one extremely important point—on the increase of concentration of production and of capital to such an extent that concentration is leading, and has led, to monopoly."[28]

This is true indeed. Clearly, Hilferding overestimated the role of the banks and erroneously identified banking capital with finance capital. He failed to see, to quote Nicos Poulantzas, that "the reproduction of capital as a social relation is not simply located in the 'moments' of the cycle: productive capital—commodity capital—money capital, but rather in the reproduction of social classes and of the class struggle, in the full complexity of their determination."[29]

Undoubtedly this is what Lenin sought to point out (although somewhat ambiguously) in his remarks that Hilferding's definition of finance capital is incomplete. Insofar as Sweezy's critique is concerned, his is one of mere distortion, for it actually seeks to undermine the inherent relationship between banking capital and industrial capital. Indeed, the difference between Lenin's and Sweezy's critique of Hilferding's definition of finance capital is hardly a semantic one.

Finally, there can be no denying that Hilferding moved toward the direction of revisionism in the years following World War I. His conception of "organized capitalism" and the notion of the working class coming to power by using as its tool the capitalist state certainly puts him at odds with the classical Marxist tradition. Notwithstanding this fact, however, his *Finance Capital* has secured him a rather privileged position in Marxist thought. He is therefore rightly considered by many to be the father of the Marxist theory of imperialism.

LUXEMBURG

Rosa Luxemburg's *The Accumulation of Capital*, published in 1913, a few years after Hilferding's *Finance Capital* made its appearance, is by far the most controversial (although certainly challenging) work in what is called the classical Marxist tradition. In this work Luxemburg seeks to make a contribution to Marx's theory of capitalist development by exploring in greater detail the question concerning the realization of surplus value.

Luxemburg's whole approach hinges on the idea that Marx's general schema of capital reproduction, structured on the basis of a "closed system," that is, a pure capitalist economy, assuming only the existence of two classes (workers and capitalists), and excluding technical progress, allows no room for the accumulation of capital and expanded reproduction to take place. In the context of such a system, Luxemburg holds, the realization of surplus value, that is, transforming consumer goods into money capital, is theoretically impossible. Subsequently, her thesis, profoundly consumptionist in nature, is that surplus value can be realized only through the incorporation of non-capitalist areas into the capitalist system.

With this, a whole new dimension was introduced to the Marxian theory of capitalist development. Almost immediately, however, her analysis was subjected to the most painstaking criticism, prompting Luxemburg to defend her position even more rigorously in the form of a reply to those criticisms under the title *The Accumulation of Capital—An Anti-Critique*, which was originally written in 1915 but not published until 1921—two years after her brutal murder by German reactionaries. Still, her general theoretical position, as we shall see below, remains controversial and highly problematic. Nikolai Bukharin especially (on whose arguments we shall depend here extensively) has shown beyond a shadow of doubt that Luxemburg's work contains innumerable illusions and errors.

In volume two of *Das Kapital* Marx formulated his famous schemas of Simple and Extended Reproduction. For analytical purposes, he divided production into two departments: Department I supplying the means of production, Department II supplying the consumer goods. Marx argued that if the system is to be balanced, the demand and supply in the two departments must correspond in a precise way. If, on the other hand, the total output in Department I is not equal to the demand for the products of both Departments I and II, accumulation cannot proceed smoothly and the system enters into crises. Marx provided a number of mathematical equations to substantiate these claims, but they do not really concern us here. The crucial point is the difference between Simple and Extended Reproduction.

Briefly, the scheme of Simple Reproduction, as used by Marx, refers to a state of affairs in which the system remains essentially unchanged at the end of each production cycle. Here the capitalist consumes his profit in its entirety. In the context of Extended Reproduction the capitalist consumes part of his profit and invests the rest into additional means of production (constant capital) and wages for the workers (variable capital). At this point, of course, the question arises as to where the new demand now comes from to satisfy the need for the consumption of surplus product in Departments I and II? Marx's answer was simple and straightforward: it comes from the capitalists and the workers themselves.

It is precisely Marx's answer to this question, that is, the way he deals with the transition from Simple to Extended Reproduction, that Luxemburg finds very difficult to accept, and compels her to embark in turn on a more systematic analysis of the realization of surplus value. To begin with, she rejects Marx's claim that the capitalists and the workers are the ones who consume the surplus product in expanded reproduction. She writes:

> In any case, it cannot be the capitalists who consume the remainder, since capitalist consumption of the entire surplus value would mean a reversion to simple reproduction. That leaves the workers, their class also growing by natural increase. Yet a capitalist economy is not interested in the increase for its own sake, as a starting point of growing needs.[30]

In addition she entertains the possibility that the source for the new demand might be the natural increase of the population, but eventually rejects it on the grounds that this would be the starting point for enlarged reproduction in a socialist society.[31] She does the same thing with those groups of individuals that belong neither directly to the capitalist class nor to the working class (professionals, artists, scientists, etc.), arguing that their wages represent a fraction of the surplus value generated by the capitalists themselves.[32] Nor, for that matter, does she accept the possibility that foreign trade may be the answer to the question of where the demand for expanded reproduction comes from. In her view, "recourse to foreign trade really begs the question," because "if the analysis of the reproductive process actually intends not any single capitalist country but the capitalist world market, there can be no foreign trade: all countries are at 'home'"[33]

Having eliminated these possibilities Luxemburg is left with only one alternative; namely, that the demand for extended reproduction comes from outside the two departments. According to her, the conditions for extended reproduction are in fact an expression of the impossibility of capitalism to grow and sustain itself in a self-contained capitalist environment. Capitalism, Luxemburg says, needs a non-capitalist environment, that is, "third persons," in order to exist and develop. Surplus value can be realized only outside the context of a capitalist environment:

> Internal capitalist trade can at best realize only certain quantities of value contained in the social product: the constant capital that has been used up, the variable capital, and the consumed part of the surplus value. That part of the surplus value, however, which is earmarked for capitalization, must be realized elsewhere.[34]

According to Luxemburg, therefore, Marx's error consists of his failure to realize that his general schema of capital reproduction simply did not correspond with the actual and historical processes of capitalist accumulation. Thus, she writes:

> Capitalism arises and develops historically amidst a non-capitalist society. In Western Europe it is found at first in a feudal environment from which it sprang . . . and later, after having swallowed up the feudal system, it exists mainly in an environment of peasants and artisans. . . . European capitalism is further surrounded by vast territories of non-European civilization ranging over all levels of development. . . . This is the setting for the accumulation of capital.[35]

For Luxemburg, capitalism is clearly an inherently expansionist system. According to her, capitalist economic expansion describes a process of drawing the non-European nations into the capitalist system. Imperialism is therefore the consequence of the process of capitalist accumulation. In this context, capitalism will continue to exist as long as there are non-capitalist regions left around the world to be incorporated into the capitalist system. Luxemburg, however, quickly qualifies this by stressing that capitalist expansion is a contradictory process. Thus she goes on to observe that:

> Imperialism is the political expression of the accumulation of capital in its competitive struggle for what remains still open of the non-capitalist environment. . . . With the high development of the capitalist countries and their increasingly severe competition in acquiring non-capitalist areas, imperialism grows in lawlessness and violence, both in aggression against the non-capitalist world and in ever more serious conflicts among the competing capitalist countries. But the more violently, ruthlessly and thoroughly imperialism brings about the decline of non-capitalist civilizations, the more rapidly it cuts the very ground from under the feet of capitalist accumulation. Though imperialism is the historical method for prolonging the career of capitalism, it is also a sure means of bringing it to a swift conclusion. This is not to say that capitalist developments must be actually driven to this extreme: the mere tendency towards imperialism of itself takes forms which make the final phase of capitalism a period of catastrophe.[36]

In view of these considerations, it is obvious that, according to Luxemburg, capitalism could not go on much longer. Crises of overproduction on a global scale would lead to the collapse of capitalism. Nevertheless, Luxemburg points out that this did not imply that the crises of capitalism would be sufficient by themselves to bring about the end of the system. Hence she stresses the idea that capitalism has to be violently overthrown by the working class. It is worth quoting Luxemburg on this point again:

> The more ruthlessly capital sets about the destruction of non-capitalist strata at home and in the outside world, the more it lowers the standard of living for the workers as a whole, the greater also is the chance in the day-to-day history of capital. It becomes a string of political and social disasters and convulsions, and under these conditions, punctuated by periodical economic catastrophes or crises, accumulation can go on no longer.
>
> But even before this natural economic impasse of capital's own creating is properly reached it becomes a necessity for the international working class to revolt against the rule of capital.[37]

When Luxemburg wrote *The Accumulation of Capital*, she had little doubt that she was making a major contribution to Marx's theory of capitalist development. In her view, she was correcting certain theoretical errors of Marx, giving, in effect, greater strength to his politico-economic project. She certainly had not anticipated that her work would be met with such passionate resistance. Yet there is plenty to be criticized in her work.

Luxemburg proposed to show that capitalism is grounded upon its imperialist expansion on the non-capitalist regions of the world. Because of this, her work is of historical significance: it forced Marxists to turn their attention to the issue concerning the relationship between the advanced countries and the less-developed world. In the process of this unique endeavor, however, she committed a number of serious theoretical errors that she either refused or failed to see. First and foremost, she was absolutely mistaken in her views that capitalism and capitalist accumulation cannot take place in a "pure" capitalist environment. Her whole approach about the question of the realization of surplus value is based on the faulty notion that "consumption does not increase as investment increases."[38] In this sense, she failed to recognize (quite surprising for a theoretician of her caliber) that the export of capital is not an indication that the capitalists cannot realize produced surplus value at home, but merely an expression of the pursuit of capitalists toward a higher rate of profit. As a result, Bukharin was perfectly right when he charged Luxemburg with having confused realization with accumulation.[39] The implications of this confusion, moreover, are profound. Essentially, it means that Luxemburg's theory of the realization of surplus value played itself out in the reformist image by ignoring the question of exploitation. Thus, Bukharin again:

> The reader will have noticed how strangely Rosa Luxemburg formulates the question of the economic roots of capital expansion. As she overlooks the factor of the search for *larger profits*, she reduces everything to the bare formula of the *possibility of realization*. Why does capital need a non-capitalist milieu? To realize the surplus value that cannot be realized within the capitalist economic sphere. In this way, the problem of realization is separated from the problem of larger profits, thus from the question of the *exploitation* of non-capitalist economic forms. A strange theoretical contradiction: Rosa Luxemburg, wanting to be ultrarevolutionary and giving indeed a brilliant and masterful description of colonial exploitation, offers a theory that, as far as the theoretical nucleus of the matter is concerned, obscures and weakens capitalist reality.[40]

Luxemburg's conceptualization of imperialism is hardly more satisfactory. In defining imperialism as "the political expression of the accumulation of capital in its competitive struggle for what remains still open of the non-capitalist environment,"[41] she conceals the fact that imperialism emerges during a specific period in the historical development of capitalism. Specifically this means that Luxemburg's definition of imperialism ignores the various stages of capitalist development. Finally, it should be pointed out that, despite her emphasis on the violent overthrow of capitalism by the international working class, Luxemburg's approach is oriented toward economic determinism. By arguing that capitalism will continue to develop as long as there are "third persons" around the world for the realization of surplus value to take place, the socialist revolution is postponed indefinitely. It goes of course without saying this was quite contrary to Luxemburg's beliefs and strategic tactics. She was doubtless a revolutionary Marxist. Yet her theoretical analyses in *The Accumulation of Capital* inevitably placed her in the very camp that she fought so hard against her entire political life: *revisionism*. but as Bukharin put it, "such is the revenge of Marx's teaching, which does not forgive critical attacks on its unity."[42]

BUKHARIN

Nikolai Bukharin—a close collaborator of Lenin and a theoretician of remarkable talents—was the first writer to have tackled the question of imperialism in a comprehensive and systematic way. Hilferding and Luxemburg were, as we have seen, interested in the general economic developments of capitalism, and thus did not advance a detailed theory of imperialism. Indeed, Bukharin's *Imperialism and World Economy*, written in 1915 but not published until 1917, is a work of major importance—as Lenin himself acknowledged in his introduction to Bukharin's book—even though it has never received the credit that it deserves. Bukharin and Lenin, together, are the writers responsible for the complete formulation and articulation of the Marxist theory of imperialism.[43]

Bukharin's mode of conceptualization of the problem of imperialism is unique. Assuming that the whole provides, to a greater or lesser extent, a systematic theoretical explanation of social reality, and that capitalism has become an international process, Bukharin starts his analysis with an explicit theoretical proposition: "the problem of studying imperialism, its economic characteristics, and its future, reduces itself to the problem of analyzing the tendencies in the development of world economy, and the probable changes in its inner structure."[44] In this context,

Bukharin establishes the foundation for an investigation of capitalist relations of production on a global scale, and therefore the material basis for examining the contradictions of world capitalism.

This line of reasoning compels Bukharin from the outset to recognize that the international division of labor constitutes the central and essential feature of the new phase of capitalism. The emergence of an international division of labor is explained by reference to differences in the natural environment of different countries, on the one hand, and to differences in the forces of production in the various countries, on the other. Bukharin stresses, however, that while the natural conditions of production remain essentially constant, the forces of production, because of human activity, develop over the course of time and eventually change. Thus, he notes that "the natural differences in the conditions of production . . . recede more and more to the background compared with differences that are the outcome of the uneven development of productive forces in various countries."[45] Bukharin also argues that the international division of labor follows its course as shaped by the division of labor between agriculture and industry. In this sense, the division of labor becomes the driving force behind the formation of a capitalist world system.

According to Bukharin, international exchange is a reflection of the international division of labor:

> The social labor of the world as a whole is divided among the various countries; the labor of every individual country becomes part of that world social labor through the exchange that takes place on an international scale. This interdependence of countries brought about by the process of exchange is by no means an accident; it is a necessary condition for continued social growth. International exchange thereby turns into a process of a socio-economic life governed by definite laws.[46]

However, Bukharin is not a circulationist. (A circulationist approach or analysis focuses on the external factors and thus reduces the contradictions of capitalism to the sphere of circulation). He is careful to note that production relations constitute the basis for market relations. In fact, his conception of a world system has as its starting point the internationalization of production. Likewise, when he talks of the growth of the world economy, the key to this process is to be found in the growth of the productive forces:

> Just as the growth of productive forces within "national" economy, on a capitalist basis, brought about the formation of national cartels and trusts, so the growth of productive forces within world capitalism makes the formation of international agreement between the various national capitalist groups . . . ever more urgent.[47]

Underlying all of Bukharin's ideas is the assumption that it is virtually impossible to examine and study a "national economy" independent of the system of world economy. Generally speaking, this means that economic developments must be understood and analyzed in the context of their manifestation in the international system. On the other hand, Bukharin's approach is truly dialectical in the sense that the formation of the world economy is not detached from the internal developments within the capitalist mode of production. The world system is itself the product of the dynamics of capitalism.

An example of Bukharin's approach is his treatment of monopolies. The process of monopolization is conceived not only as the result of the nationalization of capital but also as the consequence of the internationalization of capital and its reproduction on a world scale. Pointing to a vertical instead of a horizontal concentration and centralization of capital, Bukharin describes a process of monopolization whose tendency is to transform "the various branches of production . . . into one single organization."[48] The complexity of this process, he argues, creates the preconditions for the transformation of "the entire national economy into one gigantic combined enterprise under the tutelage of the financial kings and the capitalist state," and prepares the ground for the organization of production "on a higher non-capitalist level."[49] This in turn is explained as a result of the objective need of national capital to secure the necessary conditions for its effective participation in the world economy, which is increasingly marked by a fierce competition between "state capitalist trusts."[50] In this sense, the formation of monopolies is due at one and the same time to the concentration of production as well as to the specific developments and changes in the world economy.

Bukharin's analysis of the process of monopolization proposes that monopoly capitalism has been transformed into state monopoly capitalism. This theoretical proposition rests on two primary assumptions; (a) the elimination of competition from the national economy; and (b) the fusion of monopolies with the capitalist state. Both of these assumptions, however, need to be questioned.

It seems to me that Bukharin's analysis of the nationalization of capital is misguided. First, his claim that competition at the national level has been eliminated, so that capitalism has been transformed into an organized system of economic production, does not merely ignore the possibility of competition between national monopolies but actually obscures the fact that capitalism is by its nature an anarchic and contradictory system. To argue that monopoly capitalism tends to make competition at the international level more intense than ever before does not necessarily mean that the anarchy of capitalist production at the national level has been eliminated. In the framework of such an analysis it is theoretically impossible to draw any meaningful conclusions about the effects of capitalist contradictions within a given social formation. In this respect Bukharin's logic is reminiscent of Hiferding's notion of "organized capitalism." Second, and apropos to the previous point, the whole thrust of Bukharin's claim concerning the fusion of monopolies with the capitalist state is based on the idea that, with the elimination of different national blocs of capital, the state falls directly under the control of the monopoly forces and becomes the prerogative of a small group of capitalists. If, however, Bukharin's view about the elimination of competing capitals at the national level is incorrect (as I think it is), it follows that his theory of the state is also theoretically untenable.

In criticizing Bukharin's analysis of the nationalization of capital, we cannot fail to notice that there is an element of truth in his exegesis. That is, there is a growing tendency in contemporary capitalism toward a close cooperation between private monopolies and the state. It is also essential to recognize that the state plays a considerable role in the coordination of economic policy, and acts on behalf of the interests of monopoly capital.[51] Yet the theoretical formulation of "state monopoly capitalism" is flawed for many reasons. The fact of the matter is that monopoly capital is divided into various fractions of capital. Consequently, monopoly capital is marked by a series of contradictions involving not only the various fractions of capital, but also non-monopoly capital. On the other hand, it should be stressed that the state is not a thing but a relation. In class-divided society, the state can function only by possessing a degree of autonomy. Thus, as Poulantzas notes

> Today, as always, the state plays the role of political unifier of the power bloc and political organizer of the hegemony of monopoly capital within the power bloc, which is made up of several fractions of the bourgeois class and is divided by internal contradictions. The relation between the state and the monopolies today is no more one of identification and fusion than was the case in the past with other capitalist fractions. The state rather takes special responsibility for the interests of the hegemonic fraction, monopoly capital, in so far as this fraction holds a leading position in the power bloc, and as its interests are erected into the political interest of capital as a whole vis-a-vis the dominated classes.[52]

As real as the flaws are in Bukharin's "state monopoly capitalism" theory, it does not follow that his theory of imperialism must be declared invalid. Bukharin argues that imperialism has its foundation not only in the internal dynamics of the capitalist mode of production, but also in the process of the extended reproduction of capital. Following Marx's analysis of the effects of overproduction and the tendency of capitalism to expand in order to utilize surplus capital at a higher rate of profit, Bukharin contends that capitalism contains the inherent tendency to expand outside the confines of the national territory. "A lower rate of profit, " he writes, "drives commodities and capital further and further from their 'home.'"[53] In this context, the tendency of the rate of profit to fall becomes a central element in Bukharin's theory of capitalist expansion. Subsequently, the struggle over foreign markets for the sale of commodities, raw materials, and profitable investment opportunities for surplus capital are identified by Bukharin as the "three roots of the policy of finance capitalism."[54]

At this point imperialism is defined as the policy of finance capital and the ideology of contemporary capitalism. Following Hilferding's analysis of finance capital, Bukharin goes on to observe that imperialism's primary aim is to enlarge the economic territory, to protect it against foreign competition by raising tariff walls, and to exploit a certain territory for the benefit of monopolies. However, Bukharin's definition of finance capital differs significantly from that advanced by Hilferding. For Bukharin, finance capital is a special category of capital produced in the process of the economic links between banks and industry. Finance capital is controlled by both banks and industrialists. In addition, Bukharin rejects the notion that the export of capital defines imperialism. According to him, the tendency toward the export of capital is merely "the most convenient method for the economic policy of finance groups"; that is, "it subjugates new territories with the greatest ease."[55] To Bukharin imperialism refers to the internationalization of economic life and corresponds with the reproduction of capital on a global scale.

An important juncture is reached here. Bukharin has argued that the concentration and centralization of capital results in cartelization and the formation of monopolies—a process which is bound up with the developments toward the nationalization and internationalization of capital. The nationalization of economic life signifies the transformation of capitalism into state monopoly capitalism, and thus to the suppression of the anarchy of capitalist production and relations. On the other hand, the internationalization of economic life expresses the totality of the movement of capital, but it can never eliminate the contradictions of capitalism by virtue of the fact that the world economy is anarchic, that is, it lacks a "super-state" with the ability to avert competition and conflict. Seen from this perspective, inter-imperialist rivalries, often leading to war, are the characteristic feature of the era of state monopoly capitalism. Hence Bukharin starts from defining imperialism as a policy and an ideology and concludes that it corresponds with a specific stage in the historical development of capitalism.

Insofar as the possibility of imperialism reaching a stage whereby the international fusion of capital might result to the disposition of the contradictions of world capitalism is concerned, Bukharin writes as follows:

> This possibility would be thinkable if we were to look at the social process as a purely mechanical one, without counting the forces that are hostile to the policy of imperialism. In reality, however, the wars that will follow each other on an ever larger scale must inevitably result in the shifting of the social forces. The centralization process, looked at from the capitalist angle, will inevitably clash with a socio-political tendency that is antagonistic to the former. Therefore it can by no means reach its logical end; it suffers collapse and achieves completion only in a new, purified, non-capitalist form.[56]

Here it is obvious that Bukharin's analysis avoids the analytical failings that characterize his treatment of the process of the nationalization of capital. In dealing with the contradictions of world capitalism, Bukharin reestablishes the Marxist position and offsets his previous reformist tendencies.

In conclusion, Bukharin's fundamental contribution to the Marxist theory of imperialism is his emphasis on the need to understand and analyze the dynamics and contradictions of capitalism from a holistic perspective. His world-system approach represents a major step toward the scientific formulation of the Marxist theory of imperialism. For this reason alone, therefore, Bukharin deserves a larger place in Marxist thought than has been thus far assigned to him.

LENIN

We have come now to the last but certainly most influential theory of imperialism among the entire classical Marxist tradition. V. I. Lenin's *Imperialism, the Highest Stage of Capitalism*, written in 1916 and, as its author informs us, "with an eye to the tsarist censorship,"[57] offers the most comprehensive analysis of the economic features of imperialism. It is, by all accounts, the definitive statement on the Marxist theory of imperialism.

From the outset, in a simple and straightforward fashion, Lenin leaves no doubt that his analysis picks up more or less where Marx left off: with the concentration of production and the formation of monopolies. Employing a mass of empirical data, borrowed mostly from bourgeois sources, Lenin shows that capitalism has entered a new stage of economic development. Scientific and technological innovations, he argues, have produced drastic changes in the organization of industry and, in particular, in heavy industry. With the introduction of new means of production, capitalist production is carried on by large-scale enterprises, in the course of which both efficiency and the socialization of production have reached new heights.

These changes, according to Lenin, signify that capitalism is already in a transition stage to socialism. In addition, Lenin stresses that the high concentration of production accelerates the monopolization of capitalist economic life. Because of competition, large enterprises decide through agreement to join forces in order to obtain higher profits. Lenin's argument thus is that the formation of monopolies is the consequence of the concentration of production, the latter being the direct and inevitable result of free competition. This idea can be summarized in the following way: free competition → concentration of production → monopolies. Lenin outlines the following stages in the history of monopolies:

> 1) 1860–70, the highest stage, the apex of development of free competition; monopoly is in the barely discernible, embryonic stage. 2) After the crisis of 1873, a lengthy period of development of cartels; but they are still the exception. They are not yet durable. They are still a transitory phenomenon. 3) The boom at the end of the nineteenth century and the crisis of 1900–03. Cartels become one of the foundations of the whole of economic life. Capitalism has been transformed into imperialism.[58]

It is clear that Lenin's analysis of imperialism has as its starting point the internal dynamics and contradictions of the capitalist mode of production. Unlike Bukharin, he does not reduce imperialism to an outcome of the specific developments and changes in the capitalist world economy, and in fact suggests that the internal laws of capitalism determine the structure of the world economy. To a large extent this must be attributed to the fact that Lenin, as Jyrki Kakonen acutely observes, "did not theoretically derive his category of monopoly, but borrowed it from Hilferding."[59]

Hilferding's influence on Lenin can be more easily seen in the latter's analysis of the role of banks in the era of monopoly capitalism. Thus, commenting on the new role of banks, Lenin writes as follows:

> As banking develops and becomes concentrated in a small number of establishments, the banks grow from modest

> middlemen into powerful monopolies having at their command almost the whole of the money capital of all the capitalists and small businessmen and also the larger part of the means of production and sources of raw materials in any one country and in a number of countries. This transformation of numerous modest middlemen into a handful of monopolists is one of the fundamental processes in the growth of capitalism into capitalist imperialism.[60]

For Lenin, the driving force in the development of banks "into institutions of a truly 'universal character'"[61] is vested in their ability to penetrate the production process. As large industries come to depend more and more on obtaining capital from banks rather than through other sources, such as the stock exchanges, banks find themselves in a position of controlling the entire system of financial operations:

> The concentration of capital and the growth of bank turnover are radically changing the significance of the banks. Scattered capitalists are transformed into a single collective capitalist. When carrying the current accounts of a few capitalists, a bank . . . transacts a purely technical and exclusively auxiliary operation. When, however, this operation grows to enormous dimensions we find that a handful of monopolists subordinate to their will all the operations, both commercial and industrial, of the whole of capitalist society; for they enabled—by means of their banking connections, their current accounts and other financial operations—first, to *ascertain exactly* the financial position of the various capitalists, then to *control* them, to influence them by restricting or enlarging, facilitating or hindering credits, and finally to *entirely determine* their fate, determine their income, deprive them of capital, or permit them to increase their capital rapidly and to enormous dimensions, etc.[62]

For Lenin, the concentration of banking capital and the formation of banking monopolies is formed on the basis of the same processes initiated in industry. As small banks are unable to supply the necessary capital to large industries, or to guarantee large deposits, they "are being squeezed out by the big banks."[63] However, Lenin also argues that the growth on the size of banks contributes as well to the monopolization of economic life. The bottom line is that "at all events, banks greatly intensify and accelerate the process of concentration of capital and the formation of monopolies in all capitalist countries, notwithstanding all the differences in their banking laws."[64] Indeed, as a result of the analysis of the new role of banks and their specific relationship with industrial banking, Lenin concludes that "the twentieth century marks the turning-point from the old capitalism to new, from the domination of capital in general to the domination of finance capital."[65]

The domination of finance capital and a financial oligarchy over the economic life of the system is stressed by Lenin as the third major feature of advanced capitalism. Lenin's definition of finance capital is formed on the basis that the close relationship between banks and industrial capital gives rise to a special category, that is, finance capital, which is formally independent from the two. As we have already seen, Lenin objected to Hilferding's definition of finance capital precisely because it was identified with banking capital. It was absolutely necessary for Lenin to oppose Hilferding's definition of capital by virtue of the fact that it was established on the "mistaken assumption of the circulation over production."[66] Hence his remark that by overlooking the point concerning the concentration of production, Hilferding advanced an incomplete definition of finance capital. In terms of his conception of a financial oligarchy, what Lenin has in mind is a small group of "financial kings" who enable themselves through the "holding system" to exercise control over the whole economy. Thus, Lenin quotes with approval the words of a German economist named Hans Gideon Heymann, who apparently, as Lenin suggests, was the first to capture the essence of the "holding system":

> The head of the concern controls the principal company (literally: the "mother company"); the latter reigns over the subsidiary companies ("daughter companies") which in their turn control still other subsidiaries ("grandchild companies"), etc. In this way, it is possible with a comparatively small capital to dominate immense spheres of production. Indeed, if holding 50 percent of the capital is always sufficient to control a company, the head of the concern needs only one million to control eight million in the second subsidiaries. And if this "interlocking" is extended, it is possible with one million to control sixteen million, thirty-two million, etc.[67]

With this in mind, Lenin goes on to stress the following:

> The "democratization" of the ownership of shares, from which the bourgeois sophists and opportunist so-called "Social-Democrats" expect (or say that they expect) the "democratization of capital," the strengthening of the role and significance of small-scale production, etc., is, in fact, one of the ways of increasing the power of the financial oligarchy. Incidentally, this is why, in the more advanced, or in the older and more "experienced" countries, the law allows the issues of shares of smaller denomination.[68]

For Lenin, the domination of finance capital over the economic life meant two things: greater wealth for the monopolists and greater misery for the rest of society:

> Finance capital, concentrated in a few hands and exercising a virtual monopoly, exacts enormous and ever-increasing profits from the floating of companies, issue of stock, state loans, etc., strengthens the domination of the financial

> oligarchy and levies tribute upon the whole society for the benefit of monopolists.[69]

For Lenin, however, it is the export of capital that constitutes the dynamic of imperialism. Lenin argues that the monopolistic stage of capitalism has raised the level of the accumulation of capital into new dimensions. Monopoly capitalism has produced enormous surplus capital. Unable to find profitable opportunities at home, portions of capital are invested overseas where the rate of profit is generally higher. In this context the export of capital becomes a necessity and of decisive importance. Indeed, under monopoly capitalism, the export of capital becomes more important than the export of goods. Without it, capitalism would enter into irreversible crises.

Lenin's explanation of the export of capital shares not the slightest resemblance with that advanced by Hobson. In all likelihood, Lenin had Hobson's analysis in mind when he wrote the following passage:

> It goes without saying that if capitalism could develop agriculture, which today is everywhere lagging terribly behind industry, if it could raise the living standard of the masses, who in spite of the amazing technical progress are everywhere still half-starved and poverty-stricken, there could be no question of a surplus of capital. This "argument" is very often advanced by the petty-bourgeois critics of capitalism. But if capitalism did these things it would not be capitalism; for both uneven development and a semi-starvation level of existence of the masses are fundamental and inevitable conditions and constitute premises of this mode of production. As long as capitalism remains what it is, surplus capital will be utilized not for the purpose of raising the standard of living of the masses in a given country, for this would mean a decline in profits for the capitalists, but for the purpose of increasing profits by exporting capital abroad to the backward countries. In these backward coun-

> tries profits are usually high, for capital is scarce, the price of land is relatively low, wages are low, raw materials are cheap. . . . The need to export capital arises from the fact that in a few countries capitalism has become "overripe" and (owing to the backward state of agriculture and the poverty of the masses) capital cannot find a field for "profitable" investment.[70]

It should also be stressed that Lenin's arguments about imperialism are fundamentally different from those of Luxemburg. For Lenin, the export of capital signifies the need of monopoly capital to gain higher profits. It does not suggest that capital accumulation cannot take place on the basis of a capitalist environment. On the contrary, it is the fact that capitalism has become "overripe" in the advanced capitalist countries that generates the necessity to export capital in the less-developed regions of the world. At the same time, Lenin remains close to Marx by arguing that the historical mission of capitalism is to develop the non-capitalist countries. In Lenin's words:

> The export of capital influences and greatly accelerates the development of capitalism in those countries to which it is exported. While, therefore, the export of capital may tend to a certain extent to arrest development in the capital-exporting countries, it can do so only by deepening the further development of capitalism throughout the world.[71]

Following his discussion of the export of capital, Lenin goes on to argue that an additional feature of imperialism is the division of the world among industrial-financial monopolies. Imperialism thus corresponds to the formation of international cartels, that is, super-monopolies, seeking to obtain exclusive control of foreign markets for themselves:

> Monopolistic capitalist associations, cartels, syndicates, and trusts first divided the home market among themselves and

> obtained more or less complete possession of the industry of their own country. But under capitalism the home market is inevitably bound up with the foreign market. Capitalism long ago created a world market. As the export of capital increased, and as the foreign and colonial connections and "spheres of influence" of the big monopolist associations expanded in all ways, things, "naturally" gravitated towards an international agreement among these associations, and towards the formation of international cartels.[72]

Finally, Lenin argues that the economic division of the world among monopolistic combines results simultaneously in the political division of the world. More specifically, Lenin sees the possession of colonies by the imperialist state as a means of securing vital areas of interest for the national monopolies:

> The principal features of the latest stage of capitalism is the domination of monopolistic associations of big employers. These monopolies are most firmly established when *all* the sources of raw materials are captured by one group, and we have seen with what zeal the international capitalist associations exert every effort to deprive their rivals of all opportunity of competing, to buy up, for example, ironfields, oil-fields, etc. Colonial possession alone gives the monopolies complete guarantee against all contingencies in the struggle against competitors, including the case of the adversary wanting to be protected by a law establishing a state monopoly. The more capitalism is developed, the more strongly the shortage of raw materials is felt, the more intense the competition and the hunt for sources of raw materials throughout the whole world, the more desperate the struggle for the acquisition of colonies.[73]

For Lenin, the division of the world among monopolistic combines and the imperialist powers does not preclude its redivision. Indeed, World War I is explained by Lenin as an attempt by Germany, in particular, to restructure the configuration of the "spheres of influence." In this context imperialism, because of the uneven development of capitalism, means always continuous inter-imperialist rivalry and wars.

We may now summarize the basic features of imperialism in Lenin's theory. They are as follows:

> (1) the concentration of production and capital had developed to such a high stage that it has created monopolies which play a decisive role in economic life; (2) the merging of bank capital with industrial capital, and the creation, on the basis of this "finance capital," of a financial oligarchy; (3) the export of capital as distinguished from the export of commodities acquires exceptional importance; (4) the formation of international monopolistic capitalist associations which share the world among themselves; and (5) the territorial division of the whole world among the biggest capitalist powers is completed.[74]

It is clear from the above analyses that Lenin regards imperialism not as a policy but as a stage in the development of capitalism. By drawing attention to the structural changes in the capitalist mode of production—from the concentration of production to the export of capital—Lenin arrives at the conclusion that imperialism is an historical necessity and represents the highest and last state of capitalism. Against this background, Lenin sees imperialism as performing two specific functions: first, developing the less-developed countries and, second, undermining the economies of the advanced capitalist countries. In the context of the advanced capitalist countries, Lenin believes that the monopolization of economic life retards industrial development. The export of capital means fewer investments in the imperialist metropoles, and thus greater reliance on profits from production abroad. As a result, Lenin stresses that the advanced capitalist countries were in a process of economic stagnation and decay. In his view, these societies have become "parasitic."

> Monopolies, oligarchy, the striving for domination and not for freedom, the exploitation of an increasing number of small or weak nations by a handful of the richest or most powerful nations—all these have given birth to those distinctive characteristics of imperialism which compels us to define it as parasitic or decaying capitalism. More and more prominently there emerges, as one of the tendencies of imperialism, the creation of the "rentier" state, the usurer state, in which the bourgeoisie to an ever-increasing degree lives on the proceeds of capital exports and by "clipping coupons."[75]

Lenin's definition of imperialism as parasitic capitalism does not imply that capitalism has entered into a general crisis. Rather, it indicates that monopoly capitalism, because it is bound up with the pursuit of super-profits in the less-developed regions of the world, reflects the tendency to neglect productivity and reinvestment in the economies of the advanced capitalist countries. Indeed, in order to avoid any misunderstanding about his conception of imperialism as parasitic capitalism (cited above), Lenin finds it necessary to add the following remarks:

> It would be a mistake to believe that this tendency to decay precludes the rapid growth of capitalism. It does not. In the epoch of imperialism, certain branches of industry, certain strata of the bourgeoisie and certain countries betray, to a greater or lesser degree, now one and now another of these tendencies. On the whole, capitalism is growing far more rapidly than before; but this growth is not only becoming more and more uneven in general, its unevenness also manifests itself, in particular, in the decay of the countries which are richest in capital (Britain).[76]

There is one final point in Lenin's theory of imperialism that needs to be stressed. It has to do with his remarks on the "labor aristocracy." Lenin was aware of the fact that a portion of the proletariat class in advanced capitalist countries sides frequently with the imperialist forces against the international working-class movement. He argues that this is due to the fact that super-profits make it possible to bribe the upper strata of the proletariat. In this sense, imperialism seems to benefit not only the monopolists but also a certain section of the workers. Lenin, however, does not go into great details on the meaning and the implications of a "labor aristocracy." This is somewhat unfortunate, for it is an issue of major concern in the Marxist struggle against imperialism.

SUMMARY AND CONCLUSION

In this chapter we have examined the major ideas and principles behind the writings of the classical Marxist authors on imperialism. Certainly there is much more in those works that our analysis did not include. But the intention here was not to offer an exhaustive treatment of every aspect and issue encountered in them but, rather, to highlight their most essential points. In any case, I think it is quite evident that the classical Marxist tradition on imperialism is both rich and profound. What follows here is a brief summary of the main principles and conclusions of the classical Marxist views on imperialism.

As we have seen, the question of the nature and the impact of the structural changes in the economic system of capitalism was the central theoretical concern for the early Marxist writers. Their reflections on the transformation of capitalism into monopoly capitalism places them resolutely (with the possible exception of Luxemburg) in the tradition of Marxian political economy. Thus, for them, the characteristics of modern capitalism—the formation of cartels, trusts, and monopolies, the emergence of finance capital, and the reorganization of capital—were associated with the dynamic processes of the capitalist mode of production (specifically with the drive to produce surplus capital on a world scale). Accordingly, they expressly declared that these developments provided the basis for the emergence of capitalist imperialism. In this way, the core of imperialism was the complex economic transformations in the capitalist mode of production and the world economy.

Conceptual and methodological differences notwithstanding, the early Marxist announced that imperialism is the policy of finance capital and reflects an historical necessity. This means that they regarded imperialism, unlike Hobson, as a specific historical category—the last stage in the development of capitalism. Moreover, imperialism was understood as the inexorable reality of an intense rivalry between the imperialist powers rather than as a process of exploitation of the less-developed world by the advanced capitalist countries. In this account, imperialism was not inimical to social growth and economic development. Rather, imperialism was seen by the early Marxist writers as a progressive force in the sense that its dynamics and contradictions rendered the preconditions for the realization of socialism possible. Imperialism signified that capitalism was approaching its end. But the classical Marxist writers on imperialism did not believe that the contradictions of capitalist imperialism entailed the inevitable collapse of the system. Like Marx, they argued that a proletarian revolution was necessary against this undertaking.

NOTES

1. John Atkinson Hobson, *Imperialism: A Study* (London: George Allen & Unwin, 1954).

2. A number of Marxists have (either in a direct or indirect way) made this claim. See for example, Albert Szymanski, *The Logic of Imperialism* (New York: Praeger Publishers, 1981), p. 33. The idea however, that Hobson's theory of imperialism constitutes the "base" of Lenin's theoretical procedures has been made more forcefully by Giovanni Arrighi, *The Geometry of Imperialism* (London: New Left Books, 1978), especially pp. 10–26. Yet what is so often overlooked here is the fact that Hobson's thesis was hardly his own: it was heavily indebted to the analyses of the American socialist writer H. Gaylord Wilshire. To my knowledge, Norman Etherington, *Theories of Imperialism: War, Conquest, and Capital* (London: Croom Helm, 1984), pp. 25–60, is the only one to have addressed this point.

3. See Bob Sutcliffe, "Conclusion" to *Studies in the Theory of Imperialism*, ed. Roger Owen and Bob Sutcliffe (London: Longman, 1972), p. 315.
4. See Wolfgang J. Mommsen, *Theories of Imperialism* (New York: Random House, 1980), p. 15.
5. J. A. Hobson, *Imperialism: A Study*, 151–52.
6. V. I. Lenin, *Imperialism: The Highest Stage of Capitalism*, in *Selected Works* in one volume (New York: International Publishers, 1976), p. 180.
7. J. A. Hobson, *Imperialism: A Study*, p. 51.
8. Ibid., p. 81.
9. Ibid., p. 109.
10. Wolfgang J. Mommsen, *Theories of Imperialism*, p. 18.
11. J. A. Hobson, *Imperialism: A Study*, pp. 77–78.
12. Ibid., p. 7.
13. For a further discussion of this point see Norman Etherington, *Theories of Imperialism: War, Conquest, and Capital*, pp. 72–76.
14. J. A. Hobson, *Imperialism: A Study*, p. 11.
15. Ibid., p. 193.
16. Ibid., p. 11.
17. Ibid., p. 130.
18. Rudolf Hilferding, *Finance Capital: A Study of the Latest Phase of Capitalist Development*, edited with an Introduction by Tom Bottomore (London: Routledge & Kegan Paul, 1981), p. 21.
19. Ibid., p. 107.
20. Ibid., p. 95.
21. Ibid., p. 225.
22. See ibid., pp. 311–14.
23. Ibid., pp. 315–16.
24. Ibid., p. 342.
25. Ibid., p. 322.
26. Paul Sweezy, *The Theory of Capitalist Development: Principles of Marxian Political Economy* (New York: Monthly Review Press, 1968), p. 267.
27. Ibid., p. 267.
28. V. I. Lenin, *Imperialism: The Highest Stage of Capitalism*, p. 201.
29. Nicos Poulantzas, *Classes in Contemporary Capitalism* (London: New Left Books, 1975), p. 97.
30. Rosa Luxemburg, *The Accumulation of Capital*, trans. Agnes Schwarzschild (New Haven, CT: Yale University Press, 1951), p. 133.
31. See ibid., p. 133.
32. See ibid., p. 134.
33. Ibid., p. 136.
34. Ibid., pp. 366–67.

35. Ibid., p. 368; quoted in Anthony Brewer, *Marxist Theories of Imperialism: A Critical Survey* (London: Routledge and Kegan Paul, 1980), p. 69.
36. Rosa Luxemburg, *The Accumulation of Capital*, p. 446.
37. Ibid., pp. 466–67.
38. See Michael Barratt Brown, "A Critique of Marxist Theories of Imperialism" in *Studies in the Theory of Imperialism*, ed. Roger Owen and Bob Sutcliffe (London: Longman, 1972), p. 50.
39. See Nikolai Bukharin, *Imperialism and the Accumulation of Capital* (New York: Monthly Review Press, 1972), p. 197.
40. Ibid., p. 246.
41. See Rosa Luxemburg, *The Accumulation of Capital*, p. 446.
42. Nikolai Bukharin, *Imperialism and the Accumulation of Capital*, p. 252.
43. The same point is made by Anthony Brewer, *Marxist Theories of Imperialism: A Critical Survey*, p. 101.
44. Nikolai Bukharin, *Imperialism and World Economy* (New York: Howard Fertig, 1966), pp. 17–18.
45. Ibid., p. 20.
46. Ibid., p. 22.
47. Ibid., p. 52.
48. Ibid., p. 70.
49. Ibid., pp. 73–74.
50. This term is used by Bukharin to refer to the notion that monopoly capitalism has been transformed into state monopoly capitalism.
51. The argument made here is also presented in Anthony Brewer, *Marxist Theories of Imperialism: A Critical Survey*, p. 107.
52. Nicos Poulantzas, *Classes in Contemporary Capitalism*, p. 157.
53. Nikolai Bukharin, *Imperialism and World Economy*, p. 84.
54. Ibid., p. 104.
55. Ibid., p. 103.
56. Ibid., p. 142.
57. V. I. Lenin, *Imperialism: The Highest Stage of Capitalism*, p. 169.
58. Ibid., p. 181.
59. Jyrki Kakonen, *National Resources and Conflicts in the Changing International System: Three Studies on Imperialism* (Aldershot, England: Gower Publishing Co., 1988), p. 28.
60. V. I. Lenin, *Imperialism: The Highest Stage of Capitalism*, p. 188.
61. Ibid., p. 198.
62. Ibid., pp. 191–92.
63. Ibid., p. 188.
64. Ibid., p. 193.
65. Ibid., p. 200.

66. See G. A. Kozlov, *Political Economy: Capitalism* (Moscow: Progress Publishers, 1977), p. 331.
67. V. I. Lenin, *Imperialism: The Highest Stage of Capitalism*, p. 202.
68. Ibid., p. 202.
69. Ibid., p. 206.
70. Ibid., pp. 212–13.
71. Ibid., p. 214.
72. Ibid., p. 216.
73. Ibid., p. 228.
74. Ibid., p. 233.
75. Ibid., p. 260.
76. Ibid., p. 260.

3

Neo-Marxist Interpretations of Imperialism and Underdevelopment

Since World War II, Marxist thought on imperialism has witnessed a major shift in theoretical outlook. Prompted largely by the need to account for the persistence of underdevelopment in the less-advanced countries of the world, a new tradition of Marxist writers emerged in the 1950s, 1960s, and early 1970s that emphasized relationships of dependency, exploitation, and oppression. The notion of capitalism containing both exploitative and emancipatory features (i.e., a "double mission") was replaced in favor of a view which stressed almost exclusively the negative aspects of the system. In contrast to classical Marxism, postwar Marxist writers have argued that imperialism is a barrier in the less-developed countries. Capital flows not to the less-developed countries but rather to the developed countries. Thus, underdevelopment in the Third World is a product of the global operations of capitalism. In other words, Third World underdevelopment is due to the interpenetration of those countries with advanced capitalism. In this sense, imperialism has been defined by this new school of Marxist scholarship as the exploitation of the less-developed countries by the advanced capitalist countries of the West.

The lines of this new Marxist thinking were formulated most fully in the work of Paul Baran, who utilized the concept of the economic surplus to demonstrate that the natural state of monopoly capitalism is stagnation (arguing thus that monopoly capitalism is inimical to economic development in both the advanced and the less-developed countries), and to link economic backwardness in the Third World to the process of imperialism.

Baran's work had a tremendous impact on subsequent Marxist writers. Andre Gunder Frank extended Baran's position a step further by postulating that development and underdevelopment are part of the same process. Immanuel Wallerstein formulated a world-systems theory that conceptualizes development and underdevelopment in terms of the role of a given country in the world economy. Arghiri Emmanuel developed a theory explaining imperialism on an analysis based on unequal exchange. Samir Amin focused on the accumulation of capital and unequal development on a global scale.

All of these thinkers belong to the same tradition: neo-Marxism. Their analytical approaches have either abandoned or radically reformulated the theoretical and methodological foundations of classical Marxian political economy. The materialist method has been replaced with idealism or mechanical trends of thought. Specifically, questions related to class analysis and modes of production have been pushed into the background. Writing from the conviction that accumulation rests on the redistribution of surplus, these writers have deduced that exchange relations and trade are the key, determinant factors to the problems of development and underdevelopment. At the same time the political implications of these approaches are also problematic. They have more in common with bourgeois nationalism and various leftist ideologies than with Marxian socialism. In this chapter we review and critique the theories of the writers cited above. We shall highlight their essential theses, and argue that their theoretical formulations, though Marxist-inspired, constitute a clear break with classical Marxism and revolutionary socialism.

BARAN: THE THEORY OF MONOPOLY CAPITALISM

Paul Baran is widely regarded as the father of neo-Marxism. In his now classic work *The Political Economy of Growth*, published in 1957, Baran prepared the intellectual foundations for the replacement of classical Marxism with neo-Marxism. In this work, Baran engaged in an analysis of the "irrational" elements of monopoly capitalism and raised grave doubts about the system's potentiality for sustained economic growth. At the same time, he proposed a theory of capitalist development which claimed that the morphology of backwardness in the Third World was determined by capitalism itself.

Central to Baran's approach is the concept of economic surplus. Baran substituted the concept of surplus value in favor of that of economic surplus in order to explain how different societies create and utilize surplus. Methodologically, the concept of the surplus has served to determine the national income of a country. Its utility therefore rests in measuring the "nature and causes of the wealth of nations."[1]

In *The Political Economy of Growth*, Baran distinguished three forms of economic surplus: actual, potential, and planned. Baran wrote that actual economic surplus refers to

> the difference between society's *actual* current output and its *actual* current consumption. It is thus identical with current saving or accumulation, and finds its embodiment in assets of various kinds added to society's wealth during the period in question: productive facilities and equipment, inventories, foreign balances, and gold hoards.[2]

In short, actual economic surplus is equal to investment plus savings. On the other hand, potential economic surplus refers to "the difference between the output that could be produced in a given natural and technological environment with the help of employable productive resources, and what might be regarded as essential consumption."[3]

Baran also noted that potential economic surplus "appears under four headings:"

(a) excess consumption;
(b) the output lost to society through the existence of unproductive workers;
(c) the output lost because of the irrational and wasteful organization of the existing productive apparatus; and
(d) the output foregone owing to the existence of unemployment caused primarily by the anarchy of capitalist production and the deficiency of effective demand.[4]

Potential economic surplus, which is supposed to measure the underutilization of capacity, is the key category for explaining the irrationality of the system of monopoly capitalism.

Finally, planned economic surplus refers to "the difference between society's 'optimum' output attainable in a historically given natural and technological environment under conditions of planned 'optimal' utilization of all productive resources, and some chosen 'optimal' volume of consumption."[5] Planned economic surplus applies only to socialist economies, and receives little attention in Baran's analysis.

Baran does not really explain the necessity for substituting the concept of surplus value in favor of the "somewhat tricky"[6] concept of the economic surplus. He believes, however, that "the rate and direction of economic development in a country at a given time . . . depend on both the *size* and the *mode of utilization* of the economic surplus."[7] Essentially, this means that Baran rejects the view that the development of the productive forces determines a country's economic growth and development. In *Monopoly Capitalism* (1966), however, a work published jointly by Paul Baran and Paul Sweezy, the substitution of the concept of surplus value for the category of the economic surplus is justified on the basis of the need to examine properly economic waste—the characteristic feature of monopoly capitalism. We are told that "in a highly developed monopoly capitalist society, the surplus assumes many forms and disguises."[8] In view of this, Baran and Sweezy went on to add in a footnote:

> It is for this reason that we prefer the concept "surplus" to the traditional Marxian "surplus value," since the latter is probably identified in the minds of most people familiar with Marxian economic theory as equal to the sum of profits + interest + rent. It is true that Marx demonstrates—in scattered passages of *Capital* and *Theories of Surplus Value*—that surplus value also comprises other items such as the revenues of state and church, the expenses of transforming commodities into money, and the wages of unproductive workers. In general, however, he treated these as secondary factors and excluded them from his basic theoretical schema. It is our contention that under monopoly capitalism this procedure is no longer justified, and we hope that a change in terminology will help to effect the needed shift in theoretical position.[9]

In *Monopoly Capital*, the concept of the economic surplus is defined as "the difference between what a society produces and the costs of producing it."[10] There is a noticeable shift here from the way Baran originally defined this concept. For example, it has been shown that in *The Political Economy of Growth* Baran excluded governmental expenditure from the surplus;[11] in *Monopoly Capital*, however, all governmental expenditure is treated as a part of the surplus. Moreover, in *The Political Economy of Growth* Baran used a method of "comparative statics"; in *Monopoly Capital*, Baran and Sweezy relied on a method of successive approximations.

Nevertheless, the important thing here is that the category of the economic surplus is theoretically unrelated to the concept of surplus value (and hence to the labor theory of value). Along with the tendency to entail a "multiplicity of definitions,"[12] the category of the economic surplus is essentially nonrelational. It can be used to analyze any mode of production, since its utility is relevant only in terms of evaluating a social order on the basis of abstract thought. Indeed, as Barclay and Stengel have pointed out,

> the concept of the economic surplus is not built upon the social relations of production. It is defined in the aggregate, for society as a whole, and cannot be represented as the sum of the surpluses deriving from the relations between individual laborer and capitalist. Thus, it ignores the dialectics of production, exploitation, and class conflict which are contained in the labor process (sphere of production).[13]

The logic of Baran's analysis concerning the irrational and wasteful organization of monopoly capitalism rests upon the utilization of the concept of potential economic surplus. But what does it mean to say that monopoly capitalism is an irrational system of social organization? Put simply, it means, according to Baran, that the system no longer utilizes all of its available resources in a productive way.

In Baran's view, the irrationality of monopoly capitalism stems from the system's objective tendency to substantially increase the volume of economic surplus in proportion to the volume of investment. In other words, under monopoly capitalism the gap of the increase between actual and potential output tends to become substantial, thereby increasing the level of unemployment and the rate of the exploitation of workers. The reason for this is attributed to underproduction or to the underutilization of all available productive resources. Indeed Baran devoted considerable space to the question of unproductive labor. In his view, unproductive labor "*consists of all labor resulting in the output of goods and services the demand for which is attributable to the specific conditions and relationships of the capitalist system, and which would be absent in a rationally ordered society.*"[14]

Baran's claim is that unproductive labor does not create revenues, but is "maintained by a part of society's economic surplus."[15] This claim, however, is highly questionable. As Peter Meiskins has argued, Marx maintained that "certain kinds of unproductive labor (e.g., commercial workers) are exploited in the sense that they perform surplus-labor."[16] More important, perhaps, the problem with Baran's whole definition of unproductive labor is that it is measured on the criterion of a "rationally ordered society," as well as that it is based on the concept of surplus. This means, as Anthony Brewer has so perceptively pointed out, that "any outputs that Baran disapproves of . . . are to count as part of actual consumption, but not of necessary consumption."[17]

Baran also claimed that concentration of profits into the hands of the monopolistic enterprises has hindered investment. Because of the elimination of competition, Baran argued, monopolies have no real incentive to invest. Thus, in discussing technological innovations—a major source of investment—Baran observed that "under conditions of monopoly and oligopoly there may be a strong tendency to . . . suppress technological advance until the existing equipment is written off."[18] Indeed an underlying assumption here is that "under monopolistic capitalism there is no strong tendency for the automatic development of conditions . . . that would provide additional incentives for the investment of the economic surplus."[19]

Undoubtedly Baran believed that the laws of motion of monopoly capitalism are somehow fundamentally different from those in operation under the competitive model of capitalism. Writing in terms reminiscent of liberal reformers, Baran argued that the fundamental difference between competitive capitalism and monopoly capitalism is that while the former indeed promotes growth, the latter does not. Stagnation and economic crises constitute the reality of monopoly capitalism.

Baran's views on monopoly capitalism are both theoretically and empirically invalid. First, Baran's understanding of competition rests on neoclassical theory. That is, Baran defines competition in terms of the actual number of firms in the market. But as we have seen in Chapter 1, Marx regarded competition as the nature and character of capital. The objective nature of competition rests on the very existence of free wage labor. The facts, on the other hand, do not support Baran's claim that the natural state of monopoly capitalism is stagnation. Monopoly capitalism has been at the forefront of technological progress. Baran not only underestimated the dynamics of monopoly capitalism but, strangely enough, romanticized the era of competitive capitalism. To be sure, these are strange tendencies for someone who claimed to be a Marxist.

Toward the end of his discussion of monopoly capitalism, Baran went on to examine government military spending as a possible outlet for surplus absorption. In this context military spending was treated as a means of promoting economic growth. However, Baran contended that this state of affairs does not last for long. He wrote:

> The stability of monopoly capitalism is highly precarious. Incapable of pursuing a policy of genuine full employment and of genuine economic progress, having to abstain from productive investment as well as from a systematic expansion of consumption, it has to rely in the main on military spending for preservation of the prosperity and high employment on which it depends both for profits and for popular support. Such a course, however, while creating the semblance of a "good time had by all," amounts to a continuous dissipation of the nation's economic surplus and leads to no improvement of people's real income. Worse still, it cannot be followed indefinitely. The common man, employed and hard-working but seeing no advances in his living conditions, is bound to get increasingly weary of paying taxes to maintain a military establishment the necessity of which becomes progressively doubtful.[20]

For Baran, then, stagnation seems to be the natural condition of monopoly capitalism. Because of this, he concluded that the system must be replaced by socialism.

BARAN ON ECONOMIC BACKWARDNESS

Baran's analysis of the impact of capitalism on the less-developed countries of the world is formed naturally on the basis of the concept of the economic surplus. Baran was the first writer to develop in-depth the surplus-extraction thesis. In this sense, he was the first postwar Marxist to challenge the conventional view that the Third World had always been underdeveloped. He also rejected the theory of a "vicious circle of poverty."

Baran had no difficulty stating the *problematique* of Third World underdevelopment in clear and precise terms. The question was indeed simple: "Why is it that in the backward capitalist countries there has been no advance along the lines of capitalist development that are familiar from the history of other capitalist countries, and why is it that forward movement there has been either slow or altogether absent?"[21] With this question Baran initiated a new theoretical project.

Before he embarked to investigate the question of less-advanced economies in the Third World, Baran emphasized the factors responsible for the dissolution of feudalism and the emergence of capitalism in Western Europe. He noted three major factors: an increase in agricultural output accompanied by the displacement of peasants, and therefore the emergence of the working class; the division of labor and the rise of a class of merchants and artisans; and the accumulation of capital in the hands of the merchant class and wealthy peasants.

Of all these factors, Baran viewed the accumulation of merchant capital as the most significant one. He justified this by saying that even though the primary accumulation of capital is not a sufficient condition to bring about capitalism, it was necessary for the transformation of the feudal mode of production. Specifically, he noted that the process of the primary accumulation of capital opened up the way for industry and the expansion of trade.

Baran denied that the gap in economic growth and development between Western Europe and the rest of the world was due to the fact that capitalism was first introduced in Western Europe. According to him, this "was actually determined by the nature of Western European development itself. For the effects of Western European capitalist penetration of the outside world were enormously complex."[22] Thus he noted, for example, that Western European expansion into North America, Australia, and New Zealand encountered little resistance from the existing social organizations in those parts of the world. As he described it, "Western Europeans entered more or less complete societal vacua, and *settled* in those areas establishing themselves as their permanent residents."[23] But things were different in the case of Asia and Africa. The natural environment and the existing social organizations there precluded "any mass settlement of Western European arrivals."[24] Faced with these conditions, "the Western European visitors rapidly determined to extract the largest possible gains from the host countries, and to take their loot home."[25]

According to Baran, the penetration of Western European capitalism into non-European societies contributed radically to "the process of decomposition of their pre-capitalist structures."[26] It destroyed the self-sufficiency of their agricultural economies. More specifically, it forced them to produce crops for export; seized their land; reduced their working population to conditions of paupery; established administrative institutions to enforce capitalist relations; and diverted part of their economic surplus to the building of an infrastructure in order to accommodate the needs of capital.[27]

But this is not all. Baran claimed that the penetration of capitalism established conditions that at the same time blocked the further development of the non-European societies. The extraction of their wealth set back the primary accumulation of capital. Competition from abroad stifled the development of industries. In other words, the development of non-European countries was "forcibly shunted off its normal course, distorted and crippled to suit the purposes of Western imperialism."[28]

Baran's argument here is simple: capitalist penetration into the Third World accelerated some of the conditions for the development of capitalism, but blocked the development of others. As a result, "the peoples who came into the orbit of Western capitalist expansion"

> found themselves in the twilight of feudalism and capitalism enduring the worst features of both worlds, and the entire impact of imperialist subjugation to boot. To oppression by their feudal lords, ruthless by tradition, was added domination by foreign and domestic capitalists, callous and limited only by what the traffic would bear. . . . They lived in abysmal misery, yet they had no prospect of a better tomorrow. They existed under capitalism, yet there was no accumulation of capital. They lost their time-honored means of livelihood, their arts and crafts, yet there was no modern industry to provide new ones in their place. They were thrust into extensive contact with the advanced science of the West, yet remained in a state of the darkest backwardness.[29]

To support this claim, Baran pointed to the economic development in India and Japan. His argument is that India's economic development was distorted because it fell prey to British imperialism. Britain's subjugation of India destroyed the foundations of its society and economy, deprived it from its wealth, and left it in a state of economic underdevelopment. Indeed, Baran argued that India's development would have been very different had it not been for the removal of its surplus.

On the other hand, the case of Japan is used to illustrate the point that economic development in that country was possible precisely because it escaped Western invasion and exploitation. Baran pointed to three factors that enabled Japan to escape being turned into a colony: (a) the paucity of its natural resources; (b) the struggle among the imperialist powers in China and the Middle East; and (c) the efforts of the state to promote industrial capitalism due to the military and economic threat posed from the West.

According to Baran, the fact that Japan managed to escape Western imperialism had a profound impact on the country's subsequent development:

> It was not only allowed to invest its economic surplus in its own economy; its being spared the mass invasion of Western fortune hunters, soldiers, sailors, and "civilizers" saved it also from the extremes of xenophobia which so markedly retarded the spread of Western science in other countries of Asia. The exceptional receptiveness to Western knowledge . . . was largely due to the fortunate circumstance that Western civilization was not brought to Japan at the point of a gun, that Western thought and Western technology were in Japan not directly associated with plunder, arson, and murder as they were in India, China, and other now underdeveloped countries. This permitted the retention in Japan of a socio-psychological "climate" not inimical to the adoption of Western science both through the importation of Western technicians and through dispatching young men to Western centers of learning.[30]

What is striking about these assumptions is Baran's apparent belief that imperialism can actually proceed along a peaceful path, without necessarily causing misery and suffering. Hence in the closing part of his discussion on the roots of "backwardness," Baran made the following rather extraordinary statement:

> Indeed, if the most advanced countries' contact with the backward world had been different from what it was, if it had consisted of genuine cooperation and assistance rather than of oppression and exploitation, then the progressive development of the now underdeveloped countries would have proceeded with incomparably less delay, less friction, less human sacrifice and suffering. A peaceful transplantation of Western culture, science, and technology to the less advanced countries would have served everywhere as a powerful catalyst of economic progress. The violent, destructive, and predatory opening up of the weaker countries by Western capitalism immeasurably distorted their development.[31]

Moving into the contemporary setting of the less-developed countries, Baran addressed the issue of the morphology of backwardness by referring to the four major sectors of the economy that produce and utilize surplus: the agricultural sector, the trade sector, the industrial sector, and the state sector.

Baran noted that most of the economic surplus in the backward countries is generated in the agricultural sector. However, Baran argued, the way in which agricultural surplus is utilized undermines economic development and growth. In the first place, if agricultural production is based on large estates, the land-owning class tends to consume most of the surplus. This is due to the fact that investment is not profitable. Machinery is expensive, wages are cheap, prices fluctuate, and interest rates are high. Naturally, all of these conditions discourage the productive utilization of surplus. In addition, Baran pointed out that the lifestyle of the large land-owning class in the less-advanced countries—lavish living and excessive consumption—also slows down the productive utilization of surplus. But this attitude, Baran stressed, "is wholly appropriate to the objective economic conditions."[32]

In the second place, if agricultural production is based on small-scale production, there is no potential for an increase of productivity by virtue of the fact that peasants do not own large amounts of land. Indeed, Baran rejected the "populist" claim that the apportionment of the large estates would improve the state of agriculture.

In effect, Baran denied that agrarian reforms per se can actually solve the problem of low productivity and waste in the agricultural sector. Agrarian reforms can be successful only if they proceed with the simultaneous implementation of policies favoring industrial development. But for this to happen, Baran correctly noted, a bourgeois-dominated state is a necessary condition. Of course, what this means is that Baran considered social relations in the less-advanced countries to be roughly analogous to those of feudal societies.

In his discussion of the trade sector, Baran noted that the merchant and money lenders appropriate a large share of the economic surplus without making a contribution to social output. According to Baran, conditions in the less-advanced countries bar "the *entry* of . . . mercantile accumulations . . . into the sphere of industrial production."[33] This "lumpen bourgeois" element dwells in the sphere of circulation or becomes involved in "various undertakings auxiliary to the operation of Western business, in importing, exporting, money lending, and speculation."[34]

Baran suggested that the nature of the industrial sector provides many of the answers for the lack of economic development and growth in the less-advanced countries. Noting that "industrial expansion under capitalism depends largely on its gathering its own momentum,"[35] Baran went on to observe that the emergence of internal markets in the less-advanced countries was an appendage to the internal market of the West. The consequence of this was the stimulation of industrial growth in the West and the simultaneous suppression of industrial expansion in the less-advanced countries.

There are a number of arguments that Baran outlined in order to explain the lack of industrial growth in the less-advanced countries. First of all, he pointed to the absence of state support to protect infant industries from competition abroad. Second, he argued that the low level of industrial output and wages produces narrow markets which discourage development, and therefore investment. And, last, he claimed that the narrow markets become monopolistically controlled, thus preventing the expansion of the market.

Baran's discussion on industrial development in the less-advanced countries does not rest on the notion of surplus-extraction, but rather on the lack of investment. This shift in Baran's explanation of the cause of economic backwardness is self-contradictory.[36] At the very least, it is fair here to ask the question: which is the cause, and which is the effect? It is fair, I think, to ask this question, since Baran never establishes a sufficiently strong argument to show that the lack of investment is due to the extraction of surplus.

In his discussion of the utilization of surplus by the state, Baran noted three major types of government: colonial regimes, comprador regimes, and "New Deal" type of governments. According to Baran, however, while there are fundamental differences in the way these types of government utilize surplus, the diversity is not that great.

Colonial regimes are of course under the direct rule of the imperialist powers. Therefore, the essential task that they fulfill is to provide foreign capital with an environment that is conducive to its needs and interests. In Baran's view, even the spending on social services is guided from the standpoint of what serves the specific interest of the imperialist powers. Comprador regimes, on the other hand, such as those of the oil-producing states in the Middle East, have managed for the most part to secure better terms in their dealings with foreign companies. Hence Baran observed that "in Iraq, inhabited by 5 million people, the government collected in 1954 over 191 million dollars from the oil companies."[37] But the oil revenues, Baran stressed, are wasted by corrupt administrations controlled by absentee landlords. He wrote, thus, that "waste, corruption, squandering of vast sums on the maintenance of sprawling bureaucracies and military establishments the sole function of which is to keep the comprador regimes in power, characterize all of the countries in question."[38]

The "New Deal" type of governments emerged as a result of anti-colonial struggles. Baran pointed out that the anti-colonial struggle was based on broad popular movements with the objective of charting viable paths for political independence and indigenous processes of industrial development. In general, the anti-imperialist front consisted of progressive bourgeoisie, intellectuals, workers, peasants, and even segments of the feudal aristocracy. As such, it was held together by the national question.

Baran stressed, however, that once national independence had been achieved, the anti-imperialist alliance disintegrates. The issue of class and class interests now claim social primacy. Baran's views on the national question are worth quoting at some length. He wrote:

> While a number of important, indeed central, issues of economic and social development in colonial and dependent countries are actually closely linked with the question of national independence, there are at least as many the relation of which to the national question consists primarily of their being confused and obscured by it. Neither the oppression and exploitation of the peasantry by the landed aristocracy nor the strangulation of industrial development by monopolistic business are merely *national* questions; they are just as much, if not more, *social* problems, to be faced and to be dealt with as such. Thus the nationalist movements, after acquiring power in the newly established national states, cannot but enter a process of disintegration. The socially heterogenous elements, ever so tenuously united during the period of the anti-imperialist struggle, become more or less rapidly polarized and identified with the opposing class forces within the framework of the new society.[39]

According to Baran, the basic determination of the specific structure of the newly independent state depends on the given balance of class forces. If the peasantry and the working class are strong forces, then the bourgeoisie counters this threat by uniting with the reactionary feudal aristocracy, the comprador elements of the society, and imperialist interests. The result is the suppression of the popular movement for "genuine national and social liberation," and the establishment of "the *ancien regime* not *de jure* but *de facto*."[40] Baran cited China under the Kuomintang, Pakistan, the Philippines, South Korea, and South Vietnam as examples.

On the other hand, if the peasantry and the working class are weak, then the bourgeoisie "may feel more secure," and seek "to prevent the future upsurge of strong revolutionary forces by making an all-out effort to lay the foundations for the evolution of an indigenous industrial capitalism."[41] Egypt and India were cited by Baran as potential candidates for developing an indigenous industrial capitalism.

Still, Baran argued that while it was conceivable for some less-developed countries (such as Egypt and India) to move into the direction of industrial capitalism, it was highly unlikely that this would actually happen. Baran felt that imperialism had no interest in the development of the less-advanced countries. Thus, he wrote:

> Like all other historically changing phenomena, the contemporary form of imperialism contains and preserves all its earlier modalities, but raises them to a new level. Its central feature is that it is now directed not solely towards the rapid extraction of large sporadic gains from the objects of its domination, it is no longer content with merely assuring a more or less steady flow of those gains over a somewhat extended period. Propelled by well-organized, rationally conducted monopolistic enterprise, it seeks today to rationalize the flow of these receipts so as to be able to count on it in perpetuity. And this points to the main task of imperialism in our time: to prevent, or, if that is impossible, to slow down and control the economic development of underdeveloped countries.[42]

With this as his clue, Baran advocated the establishment of socialism as "an essential, indeed indispensable, condition for the attainment of economic and social progress in underdeveloped countries."[43] In this respect, he saw the Soviet model of development (ironically enough) as the appropriate one for the less-developed countries. More important, perhaps, Baran was quite optimistic in socialism's ability to transform the economy and society of the Third World. His portrayal of Cuba, which he visited shortly before his death, was quite positive. Arguing that Cuba was not a feudal society, because of its commercial relations with the West (an argument that contradicts Baran's earlier claim that the Third World was semi-feudal, semi-capitalist), Baran saw in the Cuban Revolution the potentiality for "the transition from capitalism to socialism—with a minimum of repression and with a minimum of violence."[44]

FRANK'S THEORY ON CAPITALISM AND UNDERDEVELOPMENT

Baran's work had a profound influence on Andre Gunder Frank, a prolific writer, who emerged in the 1960s as the main representative of the neo-Marxist dependency approach, but also as the most controversial postwar Marxist. Quite in keeping with Baran's approach, Frank set out to formulate a theory about the impact of capitalism on the less-developed countries (especially in Latin America) that challenged not only the modernization paradigm but also the views of the official communist parties. In 1966, Frank published in *Monthly Review* an extremely influential article in which he identified the weaknesses in the existing theoretical literature on the question of capitalist development and underdevelopment as follows:

> Most studies of development and underdevelopment fail to take account of the economic and other relations between the metropolis and its economic colonies throughout the history of the worldwide expansion and development of the mercantilist and capitalist system. Consequently, most of our theory fails to explain the structure and development of the capitalist system as a whole and to account for its simultaneous generation of underdevelopment in some of its parts and of economic development in others.[45]

The crucial premise in this critical statement is the notion that the expansion of capitalism contains the peculiar characteristic of producing simultaneously development and underdevelopment. In Frank's viewpoint, this is precisely what the modernization approach, as well as the established Marxist framework, failed to consider. Accordingly, Frank proceeded to develop a theoretical schema whole sole purpose was to show that development and underdevelopment are two sides of the same coin.

Frank's theoretical framework of development and underdevelopment rests on the conceptualization of the world capitalist system in terms of a metropolis-satellite structure, where the metropolis exploits the satellite. In his framework, however, metropolis-satellite relations apply not only to the international level but to the national, regional, and local levels as well. Thus, Frank wrote:

> When we examine this metropolis-satellite structure, we find that each of the satellites . . . serves as an instrument to suck capital or economic surplus out of its own satellites and to channel part of this surplus to the world metropolis of which all are satellites. Moreover, each national and local metropolis serves to impose and maintain the monopolistic structure and exploitative relationship of this system . . . as long as it serves the interests of the metropoles which take advantage of this global, national, and local structure to promote their own development and the enrichment of their ruling classes.[46]

Figure 3.1 illustrates quite accurately Frank's model of the metropolis-satellite structure.

Frank advanced a series of hypotheses about development and underdevelopment. First, the development of the world metropolis is no one's satellite, while that of the national and other subordinate metropoles is limited by their satellite status. In this context, the world metropolis develops at the expense of the satellites by extracting their capital or surplus. Second, economic development in the satellites is always greater when the ties to their metropoles are weakest. Weak ties between the satellites and the world's metropolis occur usually during wars and economic depressions in the world metropolis. Hence, Frank noted that most of the industrial development in countries like Argentina, Brazil, Mexico, and Chile took place precisely at the time when

Figure 3.1
Frank's Metropolis-Satellite Model

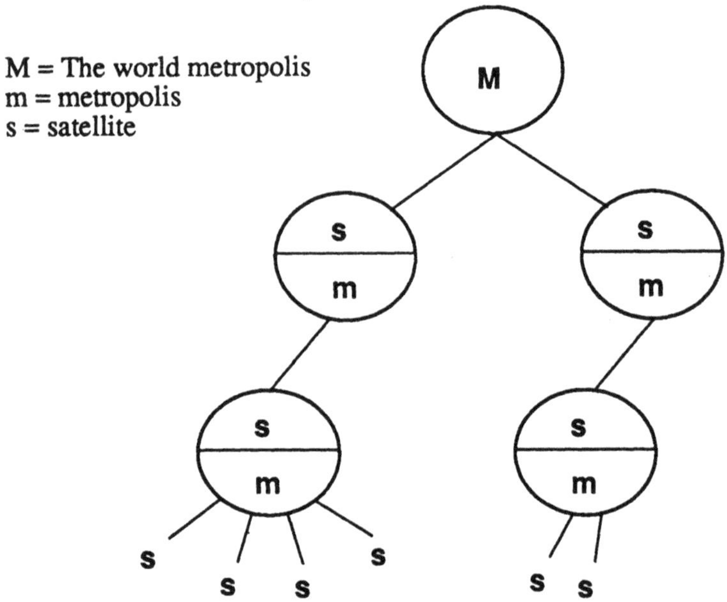

Source: Magnus Blomstrom and Bjorn Hettne, *Development Theory in Transition* (London: Zed Books, 1984), p. 69.

they were isolated from the world metropolis, that is, during the period between the two world wars and the Great Depression of 1932. But once the metropolis recovers from its crisis, the satellites are drawn once again into the world capitalist system. The consequence of this is that the earlier development of the satellites is now retarded or shifted into directions that limit severely the potential for their reproduction. Third, the most least-developed areas today are those that had in the past the closest ties to, but were abandoned by, the world metropolis. Frank cited here the West Indies, which were once major exporters of sugar, northeastern Brazil, the ex-mining districts of Minas

Gerais in Brazil, highland Peru, and Bolivia, and the central Mexican states of Guanajuato and Zacatecas.[47]

From these hypotheses, Frank deduced two additional ones. First, that the latifundium (large estate) was developed as a commercial enterprise in order to satisfy the demands of the world or national market. Second, that the feudal-like character of the latifundium is due to the decline of their products caused by the abandonment of the agricultural areas by the world metropolis.[48]

With these considerations, it is obvious that Frank, like Baran, regards the utilization of the economic surplus as the cause of development and underdevelopment. On the other hand, however, it is also obvious that Frank has a different conception of capitalism from that held by Baran. Whereas Baran understood capitalism as a mode of production, Frank interprets capitalism as a world system of monopolistic exchange. Consequently, Frank denies that the Latin American countries are feudal. According to him, feudalism was a European phenomenon that was never experienced by the countries of Latin America. Rather, they have always been thoroughly capitalistic because of their long historical contact with Western European capitalism.

A large part of Frank's empirical research and studies on development and underdevelopment rests on the model and hypotheses outlined earlier. In his most famous work, *Capitalism and Underdevelopment in Latin America*, published in 1967, Frank sought to demonstrate empirically that underdevelopment was caused by "the monopoly structure of world capitalism" by focusing on the history of capitalism in Chile and Brazil.

Critical to Frank's whole argument is demonstrating that Chile and Brazil were never feudal and isolated societies, but rather capitalist. According to Frank, historical reality is on his side. Both countries, we are told, have participated in the world capitalist system since the sixteenth century. Chile, for example, was exporting gold and tallow from its livestock as early as about 1550. Brazil was also involved from very early on in its colonial period in the export of various products.

Frank has no difficulty at all in tracing the existence of market relations between Chile and Brazil and the world capitalist system to their colonial period. The question, however, is whether market relations are sufficient conditions for the establishment of capitalism. Frank thinks so. The basis for this claim finds its support in Marx: "the modern history of capital dates from the creation in the sixteenth century of a world-embracing commerce and world-embracing market."[49] (We shall return to this later.) Moreover, Frank points out that since capitalist market relations have long been established between Latin American countries and the capitalist West, it follows that their class structure are also capitalist. From this he deduces that the national bourgeoisie is linked to the world capitalist system and serves as an agent of imperialism. Accordingly, he dispenses with the need for a "bourgeois democratic revolution" in Latin America, and calls for immediate revolutionary strategy and socialism outside the context of class alliances.

According to Frank, the integration of the Latin American countries into the world capitalist system, and the subsequent (automatic) imposition of class capitalist structures, constitutes the historical locus for the emergence of the dynamic process of the development of underdevelopment. Once a metropolis-satellite structure has been established, the metropolis proceeds with extracting the economic surplus from the satellites, and reduces them to a state of dependence. As Frank writes, then, "once a country or a people is converted into the satellite of an external capitalist metropolis, the exploitative metropolis-satellite structure quickly comes to organize and dominate the domestic economic, political and social life of that people."[50] Consequently, with the metropolis enjoying a monopolistic advantage over the satellite, the possibility for development in the satellite is erased once and for all.

There are a number of serious problems with Frank's line of reasoning and conceptual articulation about capitalism and underdevelopment. In the first place, his understanding of capitalism rests on extreme theoretical confusion. In essence what Frank is suggesting is that capitalism is born out of the extension of the market. He is arguing that the mere expansion of capital from Western Europe into Latin America is sufficient to create capitalist structures in the regions that it penetrates, and therefore to incorporate them "into a single organic mercantilist or mercantile capitalist and later also industrial and financial system."[51]

It is hard to find a more circulationist position than that held by Frank. Frank defines capitalism, and analyzes dependence, through the process of the "external" relations of exchange. In so doing, Frank ignores or obscures that (1) capitalism is a mode of production characterized by the existence of *free* labor, the separation of the free worker from his means of production, and the production of surplus value as the essence of this mode of production; (2) that capitalist exploitation is characterized by the manner in which surplus value is appropriated by the owners of the means of production; (3) that capitalist reproduction is the reproduction of capitalist social relations on an expanding scale; (4) that capitalism and imperialism cannot be treated as distinct entities; (5) that the class struggle and the state as the condensation of a relation of forces between classes exert a powerful influence on the external factors, and mediate the process of development and social change; and (6) that development and underdevelopment are inextricably bound up with different stages in the evolution of different modes of production and the articulation of class relationships within given social formations.

According to Frank, capitalism emerges in the sixteenth century with the creation of the conditions for the expansion of capital. (We have already seen that Frank supports this with reference to Marx.) From this point on, Frank associates the conditions created for the expansion of capital, that is the world market, with capitalism. But as Ernesto Laclau has noted, Marx did not make this deduction: "He [Marx] takes for granted that anterior forms of capital existed—e.g., in the Middle Ages or in Antiquity. But he by no means speaks of capitalism."[52] Naturally, this fundamental error on the part of Frank leads him to consider capitalist relations of production and indeed the nature of class relationships as a product of international economic exchange relations. Thus, as Laclau went on to say, from Frank's understanding of capitalism "we could conclude that from the neolithic revolution onwards there has never been anything but capitalism."[53]

Indeed, Laclau has launched the most devastating critique against Frank. He says:

> Of course, Frank is at liberty to abstract a mass of historical features and build a model on this basis. He can even, if he wishes, give the resulting entity the name of capitalism. . . . But what is wholly unacceptable is the fact that Frank claims that his conception is the Marxist conception of capitalism. *Because for Marx—as is obvious to anyone who has even a superficial acquaintance with his works—capitalism was a mode of production.* The fundamental economic relationship of capitalism is constituted by the free laborer's sale of his labor-power, whose necessary precondition is the loss by the direct producer of ownership of the means of production. In earlier societies the dominant classes exploited the direct producers—that is, expropriated the economic surplus they created—and even commercialized part of this surplus to the extent of permitting the accumulation of large *capitals* by the commercial class. But there was not *capitalism* in the Marxist sense of the term, since no free labor market existed.[54]

As it should be expected, Frank commits the same conceptual error in his definition of feudalism. By defining feudalism as a closed and isolated society characterized by the absence of market relations, Frank assumes that the only thing that really distinguishes capitalism from feudalism is the existence of a market. Thus, Laclau again:

> Only abstracting them [the relations of production] can he [Frank] arrive at a sufficiently wide notion of capitalism to include the different exploitative situations suffered by the

> indigenous Peruvian peasantry, the Chilean *inquilinos*, the Ecuadorian *huasipungueros*, the slaves of the West Indian sugar plantations or textile workers in Manchester. For all these direct producers assign their produce to the market; they work for the benefit of others, and they are deprived of the economic surplus which they help to create. In all these cases the fundamental economic contradiction is that which opposes the exploiters to the exploited. The only trouble is that the list is too short, for it could also have included the slave on a Roman latifundium or the gleb serf of the European Middle Ages.[55]

Having elucidated the problems in Frank's understanding of capitalism, we can proceed now to evaluate his views on the impact of capitalism on the less-developed countries.

Frank's unique contribution is his discussion of the metropolis-satellite relations. In his scheme, the key point is the transfer of the economic surplus from the satellite to the metropolis—a process which causes the "development of underdevelopment." Within this framework, the world metropolis exists as an "independent" entity that expands by "exploiting" the satellites, and thus determining their fate.

At least two major objections must be raised here. In the first place, the notion that the metropolis proceeds along lines of independent development, or, that it actually determines the nature of the backward countries, can only be interpreted as meaning that no matter what the internal conditions, the global accumulation of capital specifies the direction of development and underdevelopment. At this level of analysis, "internal" contradictions find concrete expression only in the specific features of "external" factors.

This type of argument lacks any theoretical specificity and rigor. Indeed the problem with Frank's conceptualization of a metropolis-satellite structure is that it describes a set of relations in a mechanistic fashion. It is clearly based on the use of a model of "unilinear social determinism."[56] As such, it disregards entirely the conflicts between capital and labor, and is unable to advance any meaningful discussion of stages of development of capitalism. James Petras has eloquently summarized the central problems associated with Frank's conceptual framework concerning the dependent relationship between metropolis and satellite:

> The metaphor of a metropole/satellite relation eliminates the most essential factors that account for the specific relations and processes that shape historical development. The focus on the external relationships between social systems leads to an incapacity to differentiate the different moments of capitalist development, the specific configuration of types of capital, the particular class relationships and conflicts engendered between capital and labor.[57]

Second, Frank's whole argument about the extraction of surplus is meaningless. As was the case with Baran, Frank's views on the surplus are conceived on the basis of the social primacy of the "external" relations of exchange. In this context the accumulation of capital has been curiously far removed from the relations of production. The extraction of the surplus through markets leaves open the question as to how it was produced. Frank is thus left with a theory that explains everything by explaining nothing. Because as John Weeks and Elizabeth Dore have argued, "the plunder of one geographic area for the enrichment of a class (or classes) of expropriators in another geographic area has been a characteristic of virtually all historical epochs."[58]

The positive contribution that Frank has made to the study of development is that he has discredited the modernization paradigm. Apart from that, however, Frank's analysis provides a poor basis for building a Marxist theory of imperialism. His conceptual framework is incomparable with the method of historical materialism. By failing to locate the contradictions of capitalism in the sphere of production, Frank ends up with the obvious: namely, that the advanced capitalist countries exploit the less-developed countries. As such, he never proves the causes of underdevelopment.

Before we move on from the ideas of Frank to those of Wallerstein, it is only fair to note that Frank has revised considerably over the years his initial theses. More specifically, he has accepted the basic flaws and limitations of the neo-Marxist dependency approach, and has moved toward a level of analysis known as the world-system perspective.[59] Yet Frank's analysis remains preoccupied with "external exchange relations," and thus hardly avoids escaping from its earlier weaknesses and flaws. Partly owing to the similarities between Frank's and Wallerstein's world-system perspective and partly because Wallerstein's is the most popular one, we shall stress the principal ideas of the latter rather than the former.

WALLERSTEIN AND THE WORLD-SYSTEMS THEORY

Immanuel Wallerstein's world-systems theory[60] shares many of the common characteristics with Frank's division of the world into a metropolis and a satellite. First and foremost, Wallerstein rejects the nation-state as the unit of analysis for understanding capitalist development. Rather, he contends that capitalism must be conceptualized as a world economic system based upon the differentiation of the division of labor, which is enforced by the coercive mechanisms of strong states on weak ones. (Frank's conceptualization of the world capitalist economy, on the other hand, focuses on the accumulation of capital.) Within this context Wallerstein divides the world capitalist system into core, semi-periphery, and periphery, with each zone of the system corresponding to a different level of the appropriation of surplus.

Wallerstein's work is grounded in the tradition of the *Annales* schools, whose most outstanding representative is the French historian Fernand Braudel.[61] As a matter of fact, Wallerstein's work on the modern world system operates on the same methodological and epistemological terrain proposed by Braudel. The world is "conceived as a whole, but where Braudel's approach is grounded in geography, Wallerstein's is informed by economics, specifically neo-classical theory of the international division of labor."[62] With Wallerstein, as with Braudel, capitalism is a descriptive category. The "fetishism of exchange" guides their conceptual framework. Their work is also characterized by a customary lack of theoretical rigor and clarity. In Wallerstein's work, in fact, the absence of concrete theoretical formulations is its weakest point.

Central to Wallerstein's schema is the idea that a true social science investigates the question of social change by studying social systems. As he puts it, "one could only speak of social change in social systems."[63] Within this context, the defining characteristic of a social system is that "life within it is largely self-contained, and that the dynamics of its development are largely internal."[64] For Wallerstein this simply means that "if the system, for any reason, were to be cut off from all external forces . . . the system would continue to function substantially in the same manner."[65] From this Wallerstein concludes that real social systems are either small, self-subsistence economies or world systems. Tribes, communities, and nation-states therefore do not qualify as total systems.[66]

Wallerstein defines a world system "as a unit with a single division of labor and multiple cultural systems."[67] Furthermore, he contends that recorded history has known only two types of world systems: (1) world empires, in which the division of labor is functional as well as geographically based and controlled by a single political system—such as was the case with Rome; and (2) world economies, in which no single political system prevails, but rather a multiplicity of political structures, all of which participate in the functioning of the world economy but with noone in particular dominating over the world economy—such as exemplified in the modern era by Britain and France. What is also crucial here in the distinction between a world empire and a world economy is that, in the former, "the political structure tends to link culture with occupation" while, in the latter, "the political structure tends to link culture with spatial location."[68]

According to Wallerstein, capitalism, which has its origins in sixteenth-century Europe, represents a world economy. For Wallerstein, "capitalism and a world economy (that is, a single division of labor but multiple polities) are obverse sides of the same coin. One does not cause the other."[69] In this context, Wallerstein maintains that the fundamental difference between capitalism and precapitalist modes of production is the objective tendency of the former to promote economic development through the expansion of relative surplus value. Thus as Robert Brenner has pointed out, Wallerstein's "view of economic development is *quantitative*," and centers around the following notions: "1. the growth in size of the system itself through expansion; 2. the rearrangement of the factors of production through regional specialization to achieve greater efficiency; 3. the transfer of surplus."[70]

Wallerstein, like Frank, defines capitalism not as a mode of production but rather as a world economy whose essential feature is "production for sale in the market in which the object is to realize the maximum profit."[71] The expansion therefore of the world market is what determines, according to Wallerstein, capitalism and capitalist economic development. The development of the productive forces and the establishment of free labor as prerequisites for the emergence of capitalism are nonessential factors. Indeed, as Robert Brenner has noted:

> He [Wallerstein] is at pains to distinguish the emergence of the capitalist world economy in the sixteenth century—the rise of the world division of labor which emerged with the great discoveries and expansion of trade routes—from the emergence of a system of free wage labor, and contends that the latter is derivative from the former.[72]

Wallerstein's division of the world capitalist economy into core, semiperiphery, and periphery is based on what Anthony Brewer has called "technological determinism."[73] In Wallerstein's theoretical schema, it was the specialization in manufactured goods that allowed Western Europe to establish strong states and, in turn, "to manipulate the workings of the system as a whole to suit their needs."[74] In this sense, the core states are characterized as those states that were able to develop "a complex variety of economic activities—mass-market industries . . . international and local commerce in the hands of an indigenous bourgeoisie, and relatively advanced forms of agriculture . . . with a high component of yeoman-owned land."[75]

The semiperiphery consists of countries which have either lost their status as core states or are in the process becoming as such. The peripheral countries, on the other hand, are marked by the existence of monocultural economies with the objective of serving the needs and demands of the core states. Hence the existence of peripheries is vital to the core countries. According to Wallerstein, without the peripheries there can be no core zones.

Wallerstein's world-systems approach represents an ambitious effort to conceptualize the dynamics of capitalism from a holistic perspective. Its analytical framework, however, shares the same ambiguities and weaknesses as the dependency approach in general. Briefly, in treating capitalism as a world system defined by exchange relations, Wallerstein ignores the "processes of class formation and social relations which beget change and the particular configurations of social forces which emerge on a world scale."[76] His assertion that there has always been a single capitalist world economy rests precisely on such a misunderstanding of the dynamics of social relations. The result of this is that Wallerstein's approach fails, first, to differentiate the different stages of capitalist development (imperialism is treated thus not as a stage of capitalism but rather as a "cyclical phenomenon")[77] and, second, to offer a meaningful explanation of the nature and function of social classes. For example, it is important here to point out that, for Wallerstein, the term social classes can be defined and analyzed strictly with reference to the world economy. In his framework of analysis the logic of the world capitalist system dictates the processes of class formation and social relations. All societies are considered to be capitalist by virtue of the fact that they participate in the world capitalist economy. Social change therefore is alleged to be produced within the world capitalist system. Consequently, in Wallerstein's conceptual framework, the transition to socialism must entail the complete transformation of the world system. Indeed, Wallerstein denies the very possibility of "a national transition to socialism." Indeed, it is clear, as Vincente Navarro has aptly noted, that "the political implications of this theoretical position are for revolutionary forces to wait until the right moment is brought about by outside forces."[78]

So much for Marxian revolutionary thought.

EMMANUEL: THE THEORY OF UNEQUAL EXCHANGE

Arghiri Emmanuel's work, *Unequal Exchange*, published in France in 1967, and translated into English in 1972, offers a new and entirely unique perspective on imperialism: "the imperialism of trade."[79] Emmanuel's purpose is to show that the Third World countries are exploited by the advanced capitalist countries through international trade. His work has generated a great deal of controversy, both in this country and abroad, involving not only Marxist but non-Marxist scholars as well.

Emmanuel's approach is characterized by its efforts to explain the formation of international prices by extending Marx's labor theory of value to the world economy. At the same time, it rejects David Ricardo's theory of comparative costs and advantages by arguing that the international division of labor offers advantages only to the advanced capitalist countries.

Emmanuel's approach concerning the transformation of values into international prices is guided by the notion of equilibrium. Following the classical economists, including Marx, Emmanuel rejects the equilibrium of price as "the price at which a certain moment demand is equal to supply."[80] In the words of Emmanuel "the equilibrium price of a product is that at which the branch producing this product is in equilibrium: the price, in other words, at which movements of the factors toward or away from this branch cease completely."[81]

On the basis of this, Emmanuel puts forth a number of propositions: (1) that labor is immobile, which prevents an equalization of national differences in the value of labor power; (2) that capital is mobile, which causes the equalization of profit on a world scale; (3) that wages vary from one country to another and that they are independent of ups and downs in commodity prices; and (4) that differences both in the levels of productivity of national capitals and rates of exploitation determine the transfer of values in the international equalization of profit.

What differentiates international value, according to Emmanuel, is the fact that capital, unlike labor, is mobile. If both of them were mobile in the international context, as they are in the domestic context, then there would be no talk of international trade. Indeed, in the absence of inequalities of labor costs all international differences would disappear.

Emmanuel distinguishes between two forms of nonequivalence:

> One (apparent) form arises from the mere transformation of values into prices of production, when wage rates are the same but the organic compositions of capital are different. The other, which I called nonequivalence in the strict sense, is characterized by differences in both wages and organic compositions.[82]

It is the latter which Emmanuel considers as unequal exchange. It is worth here to quote Emmanuel at some length, as he presents his argument with reference to two countries, one with low wages (India), and another with high wages (England):

> Textile production was for a long time the warhorse ridden by the first industrial country. Britain exchanged her cotton

> goods for Indian cotton and gained from this exchange the means of paying high wages to her workers. The day when India took up weaving . . . Britain changed her approach. She began to exchange her cotton yarn for Indian cotton and Indian fabrics. Then India started to produce her own yarn. So now Britain exchanges her looms and spindles for Indian fabrics, still obtaining the wherewithal to pay her workers their high wages. If India were to begin tomorrow to make her own looms and spindles, Britain would change her branch of production yet again. She would send out machine tools for making these spindles and looms. After that would come special steels for making these machine tools, and so on. . . . If India were to specialize one day in metallurgy and engineering, to the neglect of her textile production, Britain would find no difficulty in taking up the latter branch again. By exchanging fabric and yarn for steel, looms, and spindles from India, Britain would achieve the same super-profit as she achieves today with the reverse pattern of trade. Whatever she makes and whatever she sells, she must realize the advantage that comes to her from unequal exchange and that corresponds to the difference between British and Indian wages.[83]

Emmanuel seeks to demonstrate this with the following example, which compares two countries—one with high wages (A) and another with low wages (B). (See Table 3.1) Both countries begin with the same amount of total capital invested (K), but use only a portion of it (c). The developed country (A), however, pays higher wages (v) than the less-developed country (B), which means that, although they produce the same value (V), the rate of surplus value (m) must be also different. The average rate of profit is 25 percent and the price of production is 210 for country A and 130 for country B.

This procedure, centering on the question of wages, leads Emmanuel to the following conclusion:

Table 3.1
Wages and Unequal Exchange

Country	K	c	v	m	V	R	T	p	L
A	240	50	100	20	170	150		60	210
							25%		
B	240	50	20	100	170	70		60	130
	480	100	120	120	340	220		120	340

Source: Arghiri Emmanuel, *Unequal Exchange* (New York: Monthly Review Press, 1972), p. 63.

> Here, each of the products embodying 170 hours of labor is exchanged at the rate of 210 = 130 A, though nothing is different in the two producing countries except wages. It thus becomes clear that inequality of wages as such, all other things being equal, is alone the cause of the inequality of exchange.[84]

In other words, Emmanuel has reached the conclusion that workers in the advanced capitalist countries exploit their fellow-workers in the poorer countries. Unequal exchange is inequality of wages.

This line of argument rests on two main assumptions: first, that wages are independent variables (which means that wages determine the organic composition of capital); and, second, that there is a correlation between high wages and economic development. Thus, with reference to the first assumption, Emmanuel writes that "constant increase in organic composition is a structural necessity for the development of capitalism, whereas disparity of wage levels is an accidental feature."[85]

In this context, the transfer of value, which is based on the inequality of wages, results in a low organic composition of capital in the poor countries. In terms of the second assumption, Emmanuel observes that

> there is not a single example where high wages have not led to economic development, in other words, where institutionally established wages have proved to be too high in relation to actual or possible level of economic development and have had to be brought down on the basis of inadequate development.[86]

These assumptions have been effectively challenged by Charles Bettelheim in his critique of Emmanuel's work. In assessing Emmanuel's theory of unequal exchange, Bettelheim points out that Emmanuel has made a significant contribution by exposing the myth concerning the comparative-costs theorem and that the international division of labor offers "advantages" to all countries participating in exchange. Bettelheim, however, argues, correctly so, that the problem with Emmanuel's approach is that it

> isolates the "moment of exchange," that is . . . fails to situate it within the field of production relations and productive forces and to integrate it in the structure of capitalism as a world system. Thus, something is ascribed to "exchange relations" that is really an effect of the structure of capitalist system on a world scale.[87]

Given this, Bettelheim argues that Emmanuel's treatment of wages as independent variable rests on a serious misunderstanding about the complex structure of production relations. Noting that wages are the price of labor power and that the value of it also includes, as Marx pointed out, an "historical and moral element," Bettelheim writes that "*wages are not determined solely by capitalist production relations*, but are subject to a certain number of *other determining elements*. These include the effects of the class struggle and the effects of the different instances in a complex social formation."[88] Bettelheim continues by stressing that "wages, though not *wholly* determined by *one particular level* (economic, political, or ideological) of the structure, are nevertheless entirely integrated in the complex structure of a concrete social formation and are thus in no way 'independent' of this structure."[89]

Bettelheim's critique of Emmanuel's treatment of wages is devastating to the latter's overall conceptualization and analysis of unequal exchange. It will be useful to quote Bettelheim at length on this point:

> Just as one cannot "pass from the relative absence of determination of wages by capitalist production relations alone to complete absence of any determination of wages at all, so one cannot transform the absolute independence" of wages, thus, claimed, into a *causality* that is independent and ultimately "dominant." In Emmanuel's problematic, however, changes in wage levels appear as automatically determining changes in the whole system of production and in the positions of different countries in relation to each other. Hence the apparent possibility of drawing this "practical conclusion": if the countries with underdeveloped productive forces were to "modify" upward the level of the wages they pay to their workers, these countries could become "richer" and so escape from unequal exchange and "underdevelopment."[90]

Bettelheim also meets head-on Emmanuel's assertion that the workers of the richer countries "exploit" their fellow-workers in the poorer countries. Pointing to Emmanuel's error in locating relations of exploitation at the "level of exchange," Bettelheim emphasizes that "capitalist relations of exploitation are constituted not by relations between 'partners in exchange' (and still less by relations between 'countries') but by relations between *workers*, on the one hand, and owners of the means of production and exchange, on the other."[91]

Indeed, Bettelheim stresses that if the workers of the richer countries are no longer exploited, this would mean that "*their labor is no longer a source of surplus value.*"[92] Furthermore, Bettelheim notes that "in reality, these workers are, in general, *more exploited* (in the strict sense of the word) than the workers in the poor countries."[93] This is due to the fact that "*the more the productive forces are developed, the more the proletarians are exploited. . . .* This is *one of the fundamental laws of the capitalist mode of production.*"[94]

Emmanuel's approach to the question of unequal exchange is undoubtedly circulationist. It clearly reduces the contradictions of capitalism to the sphere of circulation. Accordingly, the problematic of the conflict between capital and labor has been shifted to that between countries. The inconsistency in Emmanuel's analysis of international exploitation with Marx's transformation procedure has been thoroughly noted by Guglielmo Carchedi.

In this context, Carchedi has pointed out that while Marx's transformation procedure was meant "to explain a redistribution of surplus value among capitalists,"[95] Emmanuel has substituted "branches of capital" for countries. In addition, Carchedi noted that "Marx's transformation procedure implies a transfer value (UE) between capitals and thus between branches from the low OCC (organic composition of capital) to the high OCC capitals (branches)."[96] Moreover, he observed that "under the conditions theorized by Emmanuel, the equalization of profit rates means a transfer of value in the wrong direction, from the low wage country, which is also the high OCC country, to the high wage, and low OCC, country."[97]

Finally, Carchedi correctly stressed that Emmanuel's theory of international exchange is conceptually flawed by virtue of the fact that it calculates differences in the organic composition of capitals on the basis of the disparity in wages rather than on the differences in the technical compositions of capital.[98]

In summary, Emmanuel's central theoretical point is that the inequality in wages between richer and poorer countries results in greater unequal exchange and thus to the perpetuation of inequality. In this respect, if high wages lead to development, it follows that low wages block the development of the poorer countries. A solution, therefore, to the blocked development in the poorer countries would be an increase in wage levels. Emmanuel does not think, however, that this is feasible. As a result, he recommends tax exports or the retention of "excess surplus value."[99] Having also doubts about the practicality of this solution, Emmanuel proposes in the final analysis "an incomes policy on the international scale corresponding to what exists, however imperfectly, inside the nation."[100]

AMIN: THE THEORY OF SPECIALIZATION AND UNEQUAL DEVELOPMENT

It is not easy to summarize Samir Amin's position and views on imperialism and underdevelopment. This is largely due to the fact that his conceptual framework consists of concepts and categories drawn from a variety of theoretical perspectives. Amin is truly a synthetic thinker. His work represents a conscious effort to bridge the dependency approach with the method of historical materialism. The objective is the articulation of a comprehensive theoretical framework, grounded in the problematic of the complex relation between the process of the accumulation of capital and the determination of social relations, for understanding and analyzing the dynamics and contradictions of capitalism on a world scale. Amin's major works are *Accumulation on a World Scale* (1974) and *Unequal Development* (1976).[101]

Amin divides the world capitalist system into two distinct categories: center and periphery. According to Amin, the distinctive characteristic of the capitalist socioeconomic formations of the center is that the capitalist mode of production is not merely dominant, but also exclusive. In contrast, the socioeconomic formations of the periphery are marked by the existence of more than one mode of production. More specifically, Amin argues that while the capitalist mode of production may be the dominant mode of production in the periphery, it does not become an exclusive one. Pre-capitalist modes of production are subjected to, but without being destroyed, the dynamics of the process of capital accumulation emanating from the center.

Amin's understanding of capitalism is essentially free of the inconsistencies and banalities surrounding the work of Frank and Wallerstein. For him, the capitalist mode of production is a commodity production. As such, it is characterized by three key features:

> (1) the whole of social production takes the form of commodities; (2) labor power itself becomes a commodity, which means that the producer, having been separated from the means of production, becomes a proletarian; and (3) the means of production themselves become commodities, in which is materially embodied a social relationship, that of their exclusive appropriation by a particular class—in other words, they become capital.[102]

At the same time, Amin acknowledges that the emergence of large-scale trade does not necessarily signify the emergence and development of capitalism. In this context, Amin argues that the capitalist mode of production did not really exist prior to the Industrial Revolution. Accordingly, he stresses that the world capitalist system materialized only after the full development of the productive forces of capitalism, that is, sometime toward the end of the nineteenth century.

Amin's arguments concerning the differences between the center and the periphery, however, show also the heavy influence of the dependency approach upon his thought. For example, Amin argues that the process of capital accumulation at the center is self-generated. Amin describes this as "autocentric accumulation."[103] As such, he is in line with the classical Marxist theory of capital accumulation, even though he is not very clear on the issue as to whether capitalism can exist without the less-developed countries. For Amin, however, the consequence of "autocentric accumulation" is the stipulation of capitalist development. In the periphery, on the other hand, the process of capital accumulation is shaped by the needs of the capitalist countries at the center. Amin describes this as "extraverted accumulation."[104] The essence of "extraverted accumulation" is that it blocks development.

In *Accumulation on a World Scale*, Amin notes three structural features of underdevelopment: unevenness of productivity, disarticulation of the economic system, and domination from outside.[105]

Central to Amin's analysis is the idea that "unequal development is universal."[106] Thus, uneven levels of productivity occur even in the advanced capitalist countries. However, it is most noticeable in the less-developed countries. According to Amin, this is so because, in the less-developed countries, the economic forces that can spread progress throughout the economy are either very weak or totally non-existent. In other words, "price adjustments, the tendency for wages to level out between one sector and another, and the tendency to equalization of the rate of profit"[107]—major economic forces in operation in the advanced capitalist countries—have no role in the economy of the less-developed countries. Hence Amin writes that "in most of the Third World, the rural population makes up between two-thirds and four-fifths of the total, depending on the region or country, whereas agricultural production rarely exceeds two-fifths of the gross internal product."[108]

For Amin, "this lack of communication between the different sectors of the underdeveloped economy is due to the disarticulation of the economy in question."[109] While an advanced economy engages in "intersectoral" exchanges, a less-developed economy engages for the most part in exchanges with the outside economies. The various sectors of a less-developed economy carry on only minor exchanges between themselves. Thus, taken as a whole, a less-developed economy exists in order to satisfy the needs and demands of the advanced capitalist countries.

The inadequate level of exchanges between the less-developed countries results in external dependence. This is a particularly crucial point in Amin's analysis and quite vital to his conceptual framework concerning the causes of underdevelopment. He writes:

> The trade of the underdeveloped countries, whether taken individually or jointly, presents this distinctive feature, that not only are the exports of these countries largely made up of (mineral and agricultural) primary products, and their imports of manufactured goods, but also, and above all, this trade is carried on essentially with the advanced countries, whereas the trade of the advanced countries is essentially carried on among themselves. Thus, in our own day, 80 percent of the trade of the advanced countries (the total volume of which makes up 80 percent of world trade) represents exchanges between these countries themselves, and the remaining 20 percent their exchanges with the underdeveloped countries, whereas hardly 20 percent of the trade of the underdeveloped countries is accounted for by exchanges within the Third World.[110]

In his attempt to deal in a systematic fashion with the process of accumulation on a world scale, as well as with the notion of blocked development, Amin divides the world capitalist economy into three historical periods: (1) the mercantile period; (2) the "classical" period; and (3) the imperialist period.

The mercantile period of capitalism is marked by the commercial relations between Western Europe and the New World, and the trading sections in Africa and Asia. International trade, according to Amin, "formed at that time, quantitatively, the main element in world exchanges."[111] Furthermore, "the greater part of the internal exchanges taking place at the center redistributed products originating in the periphery."[112] Agricultural products, luxury consumer goods, silk and cotton were obtained by the center through simple exchange, plunder, and the organization of production for that purpose.

The "classical" period of capitalism, beginning with the Industrial Revolution and lasting up to 1900, is characterized, at first, by an essentially equal exchange between the center and the periphery. A century later, however, the function in the relations between center and periphery, insofar as trade is concerned, witnesses radical changes. First and foremost, the export of manufactured goods from the center to the periphery becomes the dominant characteristic feature. According to Amin, "it was in this period that the international specialization between industrial and agricultural countries was decided."[113] As a result of various technological changes at the center, the capitalist industrial countries got a lead in productivity with the result being that while they themselves exported manufactured goods to the periphery, the less-developed countries remained exporters of agricultural products. Consequently, "world trade became split into two groups of exchange with differing functions: exchange between the center and the periphery, and internal exchange within the center."[114]

The monopoly period of capitalism is the crucial one in Amin's analysis of the relations between center and periphery. Following Lenin's analysis, Amin argues that the export of capital hardly existed prior to the monopoly period of capitalism. What is significant about the export of capital, Amin argues, is that it brought about major changes in specialization in the periphery. More specifically, it stimulated the economy of the periphery toward the export not only of agricultural products but also of industrial raw materials. As Amin writes, "three-quarters of the exports of the periphery come from highly productive modern sectors which are the expression of capitalist development in the periphery, to a large extent the direct result of investment of capital by the center."[115] However, "this new specialization in the periphery," he points out

> is asymmetrical, which is why the periphery does nearly 80 percent of its trade with the center, whereas the internal changes at the center have developed at an even faster pace, so that 80 percent of the foreign trade of the central countries is carried on among themselves.[116]

Amin argues that the imperialist stage was the objective outcome of capitalist development. At this point Amin's analysis breaks away from that of Lenin by suggesting that imperialist expansion was established by the tendency of the rate of profit to decline.[117] Thus, he writes:

> External extension of the capitalist market was . . . of prime importance as a means for realizing surplus value. After 1880 the monopolies created the conditions needed, first, for wages at the center to rise with the rise in productivity, as required for autocentric accumulation, with competition between firms no longer proceeding by way of price cuts, and, second, for the export of capital on a large scale to the periphery to become possible. The first of these changes reduced the role of the periphery in the mechanism of absorption. At the same time, however, it reinforced the second function, that of raising the level of the rate of profit, which was tending to decline faster at the center. This became possible through export of capital, which enabled forms of production to be established in the periphery which, although modern, nevertheless enjoyed the advantage of low wage-costs. It was then that unequal exchange appeared.[118]

For Amin, the systematic exploitation (i.e., super-exploitation) of the Third World has its origins with the emergence of imperialism toward the last quarter of the nineteenth century. In his view, the rise of monopolies and the export of capital resulted in qualitative changes in the relations between center and periphery through the mechanism of unequal exchange.

Following Emmanuel, Amin argues that an exchange is unequal "whenever labor of the same productivity is rewarded at a lower rate in the periphery."[119] Although Amin, in contrast to Emmanuel, treats wages as a dependent variable, he nevertheless maintains that a transfer of value occurs from the periphery to the center. He writes:

> Out of an overall total of exports from the underdeveloped countries of the order of $35 billion (in 1966), the ultra-modern capitalist sector (oil, mining, and primary processing of minerals, modern plantations—like those of United Fruit in Central America, or of Unilever in Africa and Malaya) provides at least three-quarters, or $26 billion. If these products were provided by the advanced countries, with the same techniques—and so the same productivity—the average rate of profit being around 15 percent on capital installed, and the capital employed representing one-seventh of this (replaced after five to ten years, seven being the average), and with the rate of surplus value 100 percent (which therefore corresponds to a capital-output ratio of the order of 3.5)—their value would be at least $34 billion. The transfer of value from the periphery to the center under this heading alone would amount, at a modest estimate, to $8 billion.[120]

Amin divides the imperialist period into two phases. The first phase begins, as it was already noted, sometime during the last quarter of the nineteenth century, and comes to an end sometime after World War II. The period after World War II is referred to by Amin as "post-imperialism," and begins with the resurgence of national liberation movements around the world.

Amin's analysis of "post-imperialism" is firmly grounded on the basis of the formulations advanced by Baran and Sweezy. The tendency of the rate of surplus to increase, and the problems of the absorption of surplus, characterize the contemporary stage of state monopoly capitalism: in this context, Amin replaces now the concept of surplus value in favor of that of surplus.

In Amin's view, the period of "post-imperialism," marked by "dazzling growth" in the center of capitalism, has brought about a series of major structural changes. They are:

> (1) the constitution of giant transnational firms that operate on the world scale, their activities being carried on through a large number of scattered establishments; (2) the impact of a technological revolution that transfers the center of gravity of the industries of the future toward new branches (atomic power, space research, electronics), and renders obsolete the classical modes of accumulation, characterized by increasing organic composition of capital; the "residual factor"—"gray matter"—becomes the principal factor in growth, and the ultra-modern industries are distinguished by an "organic composition of labor" that accords a much bigger place to highly skilled labor; and (3) the concentration of technological knowledge in these giant transnational firms.[121]

These structural changes, according to Amin, signify an end to the classical modes of capital accumulation, thereby changing the very process of capital accumulation. In turn, these changes necessitate a change in the way Marxism theorizes the dynamics of capital accumulation and crises. Hence Amin's abandonment of the Marxian theory of labor value, and the subsequent adoption of the Baran-Sweezy surplus absorption approach.

Finally, it needs to be pointed out that, unlike most other neo-Marxist writers, Amin has taken very seriously the question of "what is to be done" in order to move the Third World out from underdevelopment. By this I mean that he has dealt in a concrete theoretical manner with the issue under consideration. Indeed, his most recent work to appear in English is devoted entirely to this question.[122]

To begin with, Amin shares none of the pessimism associated with the view of the world-systems theorists who, as we have seen, reject the possibility of national development in the absence of the complete and thorough transformation of the world capitalist economy. He believes that the way out from underdevelopment is to be found in the strategy of "delinking." He argues that "delinking" is not only a possibility but "the logical political outcome of the unequal character of the development of capitalism."[123]

As employed by Amin, the concept of "delinking" does not have the meaning that is usually associated with this term, namely, autarky. Instead, he uses the concept of "delinking" to refer to the "pursuit of a system of rational criteria for economic options founded on a law of value on a national basis with popular relevance, independent of such criteria of economic rationality as flow from the dominance of the capitalist law of value operating on a world scale."[124] This does not imply refusal to participate in the world economy. It does, however, imply a policy where decisions about development are grounded on the basis of broad social and national interests.[125]

According to Amin, the strategy of "delinking" is "a necessary condition of any socialist advance, in the North and in the South."[126] It does not, however, guarantee the automatic transition to socialism. In his view, and correctly so, "socialism is still a future that must be built."[127] Moreover, Amin proclaims that the task of true "national construction" in the Third World, which is a precondition for "delinking," cannot be undertaken, let alone completed, by the bourgeoisie. It must be carried out by progressive or popular forces, since they are the only social forces to have the "political capacity to introduce profound social reforms in an egalitarian direction."[128] According to Amin, this is the only real choice for progress in the Third World.

SUMMARY AND CONCLUSION

The process of theoretical development of Marxist thought on imperialism in the postwar era has been clearly dominated by analyses concerning the problems of underdevelopment. The most prominent question in this context was that of the impact of the advanced capitalist countries on the Third World.

Unlike the early Marxist theoreticians, the most influential postwar Marxist writers viewed imperialism from the periphery's viewpoint. They argued that underdevelopment in the countries of the Third World was not an original condition; rather, it was caused by the extraction of their surplus from the capitalist West. At the same time they claimed that underdevelopment in the periphery led to the development of the center. As such, development and underdevelopment were mutually conditioned. They also maintained, for the most part, that capitalism has been fully introduced into the Third World. But the dependent and subordinate relationship of the periphery to the center precludes indigenous capitalist development in the Third World. The solution to the problem therefore was for the periphery to cut off its links from the world capitalist system. (As we have seen only Amin's concept of "delinking" provides a more sophisticated and more realistic way for the Third World to come out from underdevelopment.)

This new orientation (which has been labelled as neo-Marxism) adopted a methodological approach that was fundamentally different from that of classical Marxism. In their analyses of imperialism and underdevelopment, neo-Marxists employed a method of investigation which was in many crucial ways pre-Marxist in nature and origin. Instead of focusing on the sphere of production and class relations, they limited their analyses to the level of exchange relations. Their views on imperialism and underdevelopment are distinctly circulationist. As a consequence, neo-Marxist writers failed dismally in their efforts to explain the nature of capitalist expansion and exploitation. In fact, their analyses have generated more confusion than clarity about the question of imperialism and the causes of underdevelopment.

It is difficult to understand why dependency and world-systems theory have enjoyed so much popularity. This is perhaps an indication of the theoretical crisis that has plagued Marxism since the end of World War II. At any event, the limitations and deficiencies of neo-Marxist theory have become quite clear. A search for a more satisfactory way of dealing with the problematic of imperialism is now under way by "orthodox" Marxists. The task here is to develop methodological guidelines that are more consistent with the postulates of classical Marxism. The recent trends in Marxist thought on imperialism are the subject of the next chapter.

NOTES

1. See Anthony Brewer, *Marxist Theories of Imperialism: A Critical Survey* (London: Routledge & Kegan Paul, 1980), p. 138.
2. Paul A. Baran, *The Political Economy of Growth* (New York: Monthly Review Press, 1957), pp. 22–23.
3. Ibid., p. 23.
4. Ibid., p. 24.
5. Ibid., pp. 41–42.
6. Ibid., p. 22.
7. Ibid., p. 44.
8. Paul A. Baran and Paul M. Sweezy, *Monopoly Capital* (New York: Monthly Review Press, 1966), p. 10.
9. Ibid., p. 10.
10. Ibid., p. 9.
11. See Ron Stanfield, "A Revision of the Economic Surplus Concept," *Review of Radical Political Economics* 6, no. 3 (1974): 69–74.
12. See Otto Nathan, "Marxism and Monopoly Capital: A Symposium," *Science and Society* 30, no. 4 (Fall 1966): 487–96.
13. William Barclay and Mitchell Stengel, "Surplus and Surplus-Value," *Review of Radical Political Economics* 7, no. 4 (Winter 1975): 58; quoted in Charles A. Barone, *Marxist Thought on Imperialism: Survey and Critique* (Armonk, NY: M. E. Sharpe, 1985), p. 192.
14. Paul Baran, *The Political Power of Growth*, p. 32.
15. Ibid., p. 33.
16. See Peter Meiskins, "Productive and Unproductive Labor in Marx's Theory of Class," *Review of Radical Political Economics* 13, no. 3 (Fall 1981): 39.
17. Anthony Brewer, *Marxist Theories of Imperialism*, p. 141.
18. Paul Baran, *The Political Economy of Growth*, p. 79.
19. Ibid., p. 88.
20. Ibid., p. 129.
21. Ibid., p. 136.

22. Ibid., p. 141.
23. Ibid., p. 141.
24. Ibid., p. 142.
25. Ibid., p. 142.
26. Ibid., p. 143.
27. Ibid., p. 143.
28. Ibid., p. 144.
29. Ibid., p. 144.
30. Ibid., p. 160.
31. Ibid., p. 162.
32. Ibid., p. 166.
33. Ibid., p. 173.
34. Ibid., p. 173.
35. Ibid., p. 173.
36. Interestingly enough, Anthony Brewer thinks this is not necessarily a contradiction on Baran's part. See Anthony Brewer, *Marxist Theories of Imperialism*, p. 152.
37. Paul A. Baran, *The Political Economy of Growth*, p. 210.
38. Ibid., p. 215.
39. Ibid., p. 220.
40. Ibid., p. 221.
41. Ibid., p. 221.
42. Ibid., p. 197.
43. Ibid., p. 261.
44. Paul A. Baran, *The Longer View: Essays Toward a Critique of Political Economy* (New York: Monthly Review Press, 1969), p. 412; quoted in Ronald L. Chilcote, *Theories of Development and Underdevelopment* (Boulder, CO: Westview Press, 1984), p. 85.
45. Andre Gunder Frank, "The Development of Underdevelopment," in *Latin America: Underdevelopment or Revolution?*, Andre Gunder Frank (New York: Monthly Review Press, 1969), pp. 3–4.
46. Ibid., pp. 6–7.
47. Ibid., pp. 9–13.
48. Ibid., p. 14.
49. Andre Gunder Frank, *Capitalism and Underdevelopment in Latin America* (New York: Monthly Review Press, 1967), p. 21.
50. Ibid., p. 10.
51. Ibid., pp. 14–15.
52. Ernesto Laclau, "Feudalism and Capitalism in Latin America," *New Left Review*, no. 67 (May/June) 1971, reprinted, with postscript, in *Politics and Ideology in Marxist Theory*, Ernesto Laclau (London: New Left Books, 1977), p. 27.
53. Ibid., p. 23.

54. Ibid., pp. 23–24.

55. Ibid., p. 23.

56. John Taylor, *From Modernization to Modes of Production: A Critique of the Sociologies of Development and Underdevelopment* (New York: Macmillan, 1979), p. 96; quoted in Ronald H. Chilcote, *Theories of Development and Underdevelopment*, p. 94.

57. See James Petras, "Dependency and World System Theory: A Critique and New Directions," *Latin American Perspectives* 8, nos. 3 & 4, (Summer & Fall 1981), p. 150.

58. See John Weeks and Elizabeth Dore, "International Exchange and the Causes of Backwardness," *Latin American Perspectives* 6, no. 2 (Spring 1979), p. 65.

59. See, for example, Andre Gunder Frank, *World Accumulation, 1492–1789* (New York: Monthly Review Press, 1978); and *Dependent Accumulation and Underdevelopment* (New York: Monthly Review Press, 1979).

60. Wallerstein's intellectual task consists of tracing the evolution of the modern world system from the sixteenth century to the present. So far Wallerstein has already produced three volumes in a projected four-volume series. See Immanuel Wallerstein, *The Modern World-System: Capitalist Agriculture and the Origins of the European World-Economy in the Sixteenth Century* (New York: Academic Press, 1974); *The Modern-World System II: Mercantilism and the Consolidation of the European World Economy, 1600–1750* (New York: Academic Press, 1980); and *The Modern World-System III: The Second Era of Great Expansion of the Capitalist World-Economy, 1730–1840s* (New York: Academic Press, 1989). The basic framework and the main theses of Wallerstein's world-systems approach are outlined in his essay "The Rise and Future Demise of the World Capitalist System: Concepts for Comparative Analysis," *Comparative Studies in Society and History* 16, no. 4 (September 1974), pp. 387–415.

61. See Fernand Braudel, *The Structures of Everyday Life* (New York: Harper & Row, 1979); *The Wheels of Commerce* (New York: Harper & Row, 1983); and *The Perspective of the World* (New York: Harper & Row, 1984).

62. See Jan Nederveen Pieterse, "A Critique of World System Theory," *International Sociology* 3, no. 3 (September 1988), p. 259.

63. Immanuel Wallerstein, *The Modern World System*, vol. 1, p. 7.

64. Ibid., p. 347.

65. Ibid., p. 347.

66. Ibid., p. 348.

67. Immanuel Wallerstein, "The Rise and Future Demise of the World Capitalist System," p. 390.

68. Immanuel Wallerstein, *The Modern World System*, vol. 1, p. 349.

69. Immanuel Wallerstein, "The Rise and Future Demise of the World Capitalist System," p. 391.

70. See Robert Brenner, "The Origins of Capitalist Development: A Critique of Neo-Smithian Marxism," *New Left Review*, no. 104 (July-August 1977), p. 31.

71. Immanuel Wallerstein, "The Rise and Future Demise of the World Capitalist System," p. 398.

72. See Robert Brenner, "The Origins of Capitalist Development: A Critique of Neo-Smithian Marxism," p. 33.

73. See Anthony Brewer, *Marxist Theories of Imperialism*, p. 166.

74. Ibid., p. 166.

75. Immanuel Wallerstein, *The Capitalist World-Economy* (Cambridge: Cambridge University Press, 1979), p. 38; quoted in Peter Worsley, "One World or Three? A Critique of the World-System Theory of Immanuel Wallerstein," in *States and Societies*, ed. David Held et al. (New York: New York University Press, 1983), p. 507.

76. See James Petras, *Critical Perspectives on Imperialism and Social Class in the Third World* (New York: Monthly Review Press, 1978), p. 33.

77. Wallerstein admits as much in "Imperialism and Development," in *Studies of the Modern World-System*, ed. Albert Bergesen (New York: Academic Press, 1980), p. 21.

78. Vincente Navarro, "The Limits of World-Systems Theory," in *Socialist States in the World System*, ed. Christopher K. Chase-Dunn (Beverly Hills, CA: Sage Publications, 1982), p. 91.

79. Arghiri Emmanuel, *Unequal Exchange: A Study of the Imperialism of Trade* (New York: Monthly Review Press, 1972).

80. Ibid., p. 5.

81. Ibid., p. 5.

82. Ibid., p. 160.

83. Ibid., p. 146.

84. Ibid., p. 61.

85. Ibid., p. 163.

86. Ibid., p. 124.

87. See Charles Bettelheim, Appendix I in *Unequal Exchange*, p. 311.

88. Ibid., p. 287.

89. Ibid., p. 288.

90. Ibid., p. 288.

91. Ibid., pp. 300–1.

92. Ibid., p. 302.

93. Ibid., p. 302.

94. Ibid., p. 302.

95. Guglielmo Carchedi, "Emmanuel's 'Narrow' Unequal Exchange," *International Journal of Political Economy* 18, no. 3, (Fall 1988), p. 54.

96. Ibid., p. 54.
97. Ibid., p. 54.
98. Ibid., p. 55.
99. Arghiri Emmanuel, *Unequal Exchange*, p. 267.
100. Ibid., p. 270.
101. Samir Amin, *Accumulation on a World Scale* (New York: Monthly Review Press, 1974); *Unequal Development* (New York: Monthly Review Press, 1976).
102. See Samir Amin, *Unequal Development*, p. 60.
103. See ibid., pp. 76–78.
104. See ibid., pp. 191–97.
105. See Samir Amin, *Accumulation on a World Scale*, p. 15.
106. Samir Amin, *Class and Nation* (New York: Monthly Review Press, 1980), p. 2.
107. Samir Amin, *Accumulation on a World Scale*, p. 15.
108. Ibid., p. 15.
109. Ibid., p. 16.
110. Ibid., p. 17.
111. Ibid., p. 40.
112. Ibid., p. 40.
113. Ibid., p. 41.
114. Ibid., p. 41.
115. Ibid., p. 42.
116. Ibid., p. 42.
117. This point concerning the difference between Amin and Lenin is made by Charles A. Barone in *Marxist Thought on Imperialism*, p. 126.
118. Samir Amin, *Unequal Development*, p. 188.
119. Ibid., p. 149.
120. Ibid., p. 143.
121. Ibid., p. 189.
122. See Samir Amin, *Delinking: Towards a Polycentric World* (London: Zed Books, 1990).
123. Ibid., p. xiv.
124. Ibid., p. 62.
125. The strategy of "delinking," along with other strategies of development, has also been addressed in a clear and concise fashion in James H. Mittelman, *Out from Underdevelopment: Prospects for the Third World* (New York: St. Martin's Press, 1988).
126. See Samir Amin, *Delinking*, p. xiv.
127. Ibid., p. xiv.
128. Ibid., p. 60.

4

New Developments and Directions in the Marxist Theories of Imperialism

This chapter is devoted to a review of recent trends in Marxist thought on imperialism aimed at generating alternative frameworks which go beyond notions of underdevelopment and dependency by emphasizing instead relations of production, class analysis, and capital accumulation. In fact, various approaches have been articulated since the early 1970s with the intent of analyzing and understanding capitalist imperialism from a methodological point of view that is more consistent with the assumptions and postulates of classical Marxism.

Among the most important recent theoretical trends are the modes of productions approach, and the internationalization of capital. These approaches constitute the focus of this chapter. Before doing so, however, we shall proceed to discuss the contributions of Bill Warren, who initiated a return to classical Marxism by challenging the claims of the dependency approach that capitalist imperialism is the cause of underdevelopment in the Third World.

WARREN'S THESES

In an article entitled "Imperialism and Capitalist Industrialization,"[1] which has received much acclaim as well as widespread criticism, Warren put forward certain theses with reference to imperialism and capitalist industrialization in the Third World.

They are as follows: (a) capitalist development in the Third World has made significant progress since the end of World War II; (b) internal factors, rather than imperialism, are the chief obstacles in the development of the Third World; and, (c) that imperialism is on the decline. What is even more striking about these theses is that they are articulated within the framework of an analysis which is based primarily on the construction of massive empirical data. However, we shall argue here that the results of Warren's challenging endeavor are truly mixed. Specifically, he is quite successful, on the one hand, in drawing attention to the fact that neo-Marxist theories of underdevelopment ignore the dialectics of capitalist expansion and simply posit the existence of underdevelopment. On the other hand, his analytical framework contains many theoretical deficiencies and has an explicitly linear (and thus non-dialectical) view of social development.

In his attempt to show that capitalist development has been (and is) taking place in various countries of the Third World, Warren starts off by emphasizing the growth of manufacturing output. He offers the following statistics in Table 4.1 as concrete evidence in support of his claim.

In the light of these "facts," Warren claims that "the really unique feature of the post-war industrialization advance in the Third World taken as a whole, is its sustained momentum over a period longer than any previously recorded."[2] Indeed, Warren argues that the proportion of gross domestic product (GDP) generated by manufacturing in the countries of the Third World compares quite well with that in the developed capitalist countries. Specifically, he notes that "for the underdeveloped countries as a whole the proportion of gross domestic product accounted for by manufacturing rose from 14.5 percent in 1950–4 to 17.9 percent in 1960–4, while in the developed capitalist countries during 1960–4 manufacturing contributed 31.3 percent to GDP."[3] Subsequently, Warren goes on to exclaim that "the proportion in underdeveloped countries is already over half that of the developed ones."[4]

Table 4.1
Annual Average Rates of Growth of Manufacturing for Selected Countries, 1951–1968

Brazil	7.8	Panama	14.2
Costa Rica	9.7	Peru	7.5
Iran	11.2	Philippines	8.5
Iraq	6.8	Puerto Rico	6.5
Jamaica	5.0	Singapore	14.8
Jordan	15.2	Taiwan	16.1
Korea (Rep. of)	16.9	Thailand	8.7
Malaysia	6.4	Trinidad & Tobago	10.0
Mexica	7.4	Turkey	11.5
Nicaragua	7.6	Venezuela	10.5
Pakistan	15.0	Zambia	13.8

Source: Bill Warren, "Imperialism and Capitalist Industrialization," *New Left Review* no. 81 (September-October 1973), p. 6.

Warren's method of analysis is based on bad science. It appears that, in his eagerness to disprove stagnationist and underdevelopment theories of imperialism, Warren has not realized that "facts" never speak for themselves. To be sure, crude empiricism is the underlying guide of his analysis. As a result, Warren commits a number of cardinal errors that, in the final analysis, undermine his effort to argue that capitalist development (which is loosely defined as industrialization) is taking place in the Third World.

First of all, the key problem with Warren's analysis is that it fails to distinguish between economic growth and economic development. More specifically, his analysis is reminiscent of modernization theory by virtue of the fact that it takes for granted the question as to whether real structural changes have taken place in the economies of the Third World countries. For example, in citing figures for the annual average rates of manufacturing growth for selected Third World countries, Warren never deals with the issue of backward and forward linkages. Many industries in the Third World are controlled by the major imperialist centers. In addition, as many of his critics have correctly observed, "the majority of countries in the Third World are . . . prisoners of the international credit system, dominated as it is by the metropolitan states and their banks."[5] Furthermore, it is also true that "much of this industrialization is simply transitional; metropolitan capital builds factories in pursuit of tax benefits, cheap and captive labor, and the incentives it receives from local despots; profits are quick, and in case the despots begin to fall, disinvestment can be rapid."[6] Warren's analysis fails to address these realities.

By any reasonable standard Warren's method of relying on the growth of manufacturing as proof of industrialization is quite naive. On the basis of this, one would have to conclude then that Zambia, for instance, is more industrialized than Brazil, since it has experienced (at least during the period cited) larger annual rates of manufacturing growth than the latter.

This criticism is not intended to suggest that capitalist development is not taking place in the Third World or that dependence is a structural condition in which its self-perpetuation is almost guaranteed. Capitalist development has been experienced by a number of "peripheral" countries, the most obvious and interesting case being that of Korea.[7] In terms of the problem of the self-perpetuation of dependency, we have here a rather interesting situation. As it has been pointed out, for example, "dependent development does create investment opportunities for indigenous firms. It is not . . . beyond the realm of the possible that such companies might profit and grow sufficiently to be able to compete successfully even among the giants of the international economy."[8] But it seems to me that the point of central importance here, which is precisely the one which Warren's analysis neglects to investigate, is the actual type of industrialization, the specific form of capitalist development that is taking place in the Third World. It is not an exaggeration to say that Warren's analysis has been confined to mere descriptions that are virtually meaningless precisely because they do not occupy any theoretical or contextual space. Warren generalizes industrial development in the sense that he reduces it to the mere existence of "factories."

The same kind of conceptual confusion also surrounds Warren's explanation of the specific factors responsible for the creation of the conditions leading to the so-called "rapid and widespread" industrialization in the Third World. Here Warren identifies political independence and certain objective changes in the world economy (East-West rivalry and inter-imperialism rivalries) as the key factors that stimulated the processes of capitalist industrialization.[9] However, these views suffer once again from the absence of any theoretical conceptualization of the dynamics and contradictions of capital accumulation. In this context, Warren's broad generalization that "'stagnation' in the Third World is largely a myth"[10] may be indeed true, but certainly does not enhance our understanding of Third World development.

Underlying Warren's premises about capitalist development in the Third World is his unmistakably supportive and favorable view toward imperialism. Warren's analysis shows clearly the overpowering influence of an essentially teleological system of thought in which imperialism is associated, or perhaps even identified, with progress. In his book titled *Imperialism: The Pioneer of Capitalism*,[11] Warren goes so far as to claim that this idea was central to Marx's whole development of socialist theory, and chastises Lenin for having initiated a conceptual and political break from it.[12] Yet this does not mean that Warren is ignorant of the fact that imperialism is above all a system of exploitation, domination, and inequality. He admits so much himself.[13] What he essentially objects to, however, is the idea that imperialism is responsible for the plight of the Third World. On this issue, he confronts head-on the very premise and the essence of the analytical framework of underdevelopment. He writes:

> The theory of imperialism as a system for draining surplus value from the periphery to the centre has, of course, exactly the same defect as the popular equation of debt with a debt problem—that in comparing inward capital flows with the resulting outward flow of interest and profit what exactly is done with the capital "in between" . . . is ignored. Even if a large excess of outward flow of funds over inward investment can be shown (as it frequently can) this proves nothing

> whatsoever, either about a drain of foreign exchange (because the investment may expand capacity which produces exports or saves imports) or about a drain of surplus value (the investment may expand productive investment and thus the surplus, but in a form which is not readily convertible into net additional foreign exchange). The so-called drain may merely be the foreign exchange price paid for the establishment of productive facilities.[14]

From this passage it is obvious that Warren finds little value in the whole surplus-extraction thesis. More important, Warren feels that foreign investment encourages rather than suppresses indigenous capitalist development. As such, his contention is that the problems of development that many Third World countries are faced with are related for the most part to the internal contradictions of the countries in question. But, typically, no effort is made by Warren to provide us with an explanatory framework that will promote an understanding of this.

Finally, Warren contends that "imperialism declines as capitalism grows."[15] This assumption is based on the schematic idea that imperialism is a temporary historical phenomenon, functioning mainly as a vehicle toward the spread of capitalism. From this premise, then, the spread of "national capitalisms" throughout the world provides the basis for the elimination of imperialism. In a word, it seems, as McMichael, Petras, and Rhodes have pointed out, that, according to Warren's conceptual framework, it is "nationalism" rather than "revolutionary struggle" that serves as the "gravedigger" of imperialism.[16]

This particular conception of imperialism and its relationship to capitalism is indeed vague and confusing. However, it should be stressed that, in his effort to highlight specific politico-strategic considerations for the left toward its struggle against imperialism, Warren makes a fundamentally correct point by noting that socialist forces "must be able to distinguish inter-capitalist quarrels and bargaining, from anti-imperialism."[17] An anti-imperialist struggle in itself will not necessarily advance the interests of the working class and the peasantry.

Warren's contribution to the subject of Marxist thought on imperialism should not be overlooked. He has challenged the theoretical approaches founded on the notions of underdevelopment and dependency, and has shifted in turn attention to the dynamics of capitalist expansion. But, as we have argued, his analytical framework is quite limited, if not flawed. His theses on "imperialism and capitalist industrialization" are built on the basis of formal empiricism and on a rather one-sided, deterministic view of social development. Needless to say, a Marxist theory of imperialism cannot be modeled on such grounds.

THE MODES OF PRODUCTION APPROACH

In recent years the modes of production approach has emerged as one of the major theoretical trends in Marxist scholarship on imperialism. As will be seen, various authors have focused their attention on the analytical construct of the mode of production as the basic but essential element for understanding and explaining social development. To be sure, the modes of production approach was vital to Marx's own specific methodological orientation. Marx, we know, considered the structural character of the mode of production as the most important factor, the precondition, for explaining paths of social development. Thus, in his discussions about the development of world commerce, Marx stressed that the extent to which its spread causes the dissolution of the old mode of production and brings about a new mode of production depends on the character and internal structure of the old mode of production itself.[18] In fact, classical Marxism in general has always maintained that internal relations determine international developments. However, the formulation of the modes of production approach had been degenerated by Stalinist Marxism into a deterministic formula, in which historical development was seen in terms of the evolutionary succession of modes of production. In other words, in contrast to classical Marxism, Stalinist Marxism held an evolutionist and mechanical conception of history and social development. But since the demise of Stalinism, the modes of production approach has been given a new life.

Contemporary theoretical discourse about modes of production or, more precisely, the articulation of modes of production, has its origin in the work of French structuralist Marxists, most notably that of Louis Althusser and Etienne Balibar.[19] As conceptualized by Balibar, in particular, whose theoretical task was the construction of a *general* theory of modes of production, the concept of the mode of production refers to a theoretical construct positing a conceptual correspondence between forces of production and relations of production. The term "articulation," on the other hand, refers to the idea of a combination or a "coexistence" of different modes of production.

Balibar presented a series of invariant elements, "the specific combination of which produces different forms of the mode of production."[20] These elements are: (1) laborer; (2) means of production—(i) object of labor, and (ii) means of labor; (3) non-laborer. These elements are linked together by two distinct connections: (A) property connection; and (B) real or material appropriation connection.[21] However, Balibar stressed that it is not enough "merely to specify the variants in the combinations of elements set above."[22] Thus, Balibar proceeded to sketch not merely a theory of transition but a theory of reproduction, since it is the latter that "ensures the successive continuity of production itself."[23]

Nevertheless, Balibar's formulation of the modes of production approach has been criticized on a number of grounds, ranging from deficiencies in the overall theoretical framework to its lack of application to concrete historical instances.[24] Even so, Balibar's contribution is quite significant, especially since it generated so much interest around the modes of production approach.

Of much significance here are also the formulations of Ernesto Laclau, who presented the approach of the articulation of different modes of production to the case of Latin America in his critique of Frank's theory of the development of underdevelopment. Arguing that the system of feudalism and capitalism coexist in Latin American social formations, Laclau proposed a theoretical model that had as its focus of analysis the relations of productions and capital accumulation. Within this context Laclau distinguished between a mode of production and an economic system. A mode of production was designated as

> the logical and mutually co-ordinated articulation of: 1. a determinate type of ownership of the means of production; 2. a determinate form of appropriation of the economic surplus; 3. a determinate degree of development of the division of labor; 4. a determinate level of development of the productive forces.[25]

An economic system, on the other hand, was designated as

> the mutual relations between the different sectors of the economy, or between different productive units, whether on a regional, national or world scale. . . . An economic system can include, as constitutive elements, different modes of production—provided always that we define it as a whole, that is, by proceeding from the element or law of motion that establishes the unity of its different manifestations.[26]

Given these propositions, Laclau argued that the world capitalist system contains a number of different modes of production. In order then to understand and explain the causes of underdevelopment, Laclau stressed, one had to analyze the articulation of the modes of production in a given economy.

The writer, however, who has been credited with having developed in a systematic way the theory of the articulation of modes of production is the French Marxist anthropologist Pierre-Philippe Rey.[27] Briefly, Rey's theoretical project is to construct a conceptual framework with an adequate basis for understanding both European capitalism as well as the development of the Third

World. In Rey's view, the key to theorization about articulation is the understanding of the transition from feudalism to capitalism. The objective is "seeing exactly what was specific to the feudal mode which enabled capitalism to grow out of it, but that at a certain stage the nascent capitalist class would be able to throw off the alliance with the old feudal ruling class."[28]

Rey divides articulation into "three stages in the transition of feudalism to capitalism, and he generalizes these stages to the relationship between capitalist and non-capitalist modes of production in the era of imperialism."[29] In the first stage, the traditional mode of production remains dominant, even though capitalism draws material from it. In this sense, the exchange relations reinforce the precapitalist mode of production rather than promote capitalist relations of production. In the second stage, capitalism becomes the dominant mode of production, and the other modes of production are modified on the basis of capitalism. Peasant agriculture and handicrafts, for example, are first transformed and then completely eliminated, and a labor force emerges. The third stage of capitalism is established once the system has managed to ensure its own labor supply. According to Rey, the Third World has yet to reach the third stage.[30]

Rey's approach does not suggest that the course of capitalist development in the Third World is going to follow the same as that experienced by Western Europe. On the contrary, Rey argues that the transition to capitalism in Third World social formations is different precisely because the system is imported from abroad. Thus, the question of violence plays an extremely crucial role in Rey's analytical framework. For instance, while Rey argues that the articulation is peaceful in the case of feudalism, this is not so in the case concerning the articulation between capitalist and pre-capitalist modes of production. Here the articulation is both a violent and a prolonged process.[31]

The foundation of Rey's treatment of the articulation of the modes of production leads directly to the idea that capitalism in the Third World exists in connection with other pre-capitalist modes of production. From the point of view of Rey's conceptual framework, therefore, the view that the Third World is underdeveloped rests on a fundamentally incorrect assumption. This is because the transition of the Third World to capitalism is as yet incomplete. In this sense, the test for capitalist development rests with the destruction of pre-capitalist modes of production.

The approach of the articulation of modes of production clearly contains important aspects toward the formulation of a Marxist theory of capitalist development. But it is also clear, however, that at this point there are still too many unresolved questions. More specifically, there is no agreement among Marxist scholars on "the contents (or elements) of a mode of production, its conceptual boundary (or theoretical scope), and the manner of its reproduction (or lack of reproduction)."[32] In addition, it appears to be extremely difficult to verify different modes of production. Blomstrom and Hettne have captured this problem quite well when they write as follows:

> We do not see the modes of production concretely manifested until we use the concept of articulation, but on that level of analysis these modes are no longer recognizable because of their intermixing. When an author claims to be studying a formation which consists of modes of production A, B and C, is there any way for the reader to verify that it really is a question of modes A, B and C, and not B, C and D? Or if one anthropologist, after having studied some valley in the Andes, finds that this social formation (A+B+C) is dominated by mode of production A, and if another anthropologist, after a later "restudy" finds B to be the dominant mode of production, are we then to assume that this social formation has changed, or could it be that one of the two anthropologists has a preconceived idea about which mode of production ought to be dominant?[33]

THE THEORY OF THE INTERNATIONALIZATION OF CAPITAL

The internationalization of capital represents another major trend in recent Marxist thought on imperialism. This particular approach is also highly abstract with the primary starting point of analysis being directed toward "the basic laws of capitalist accumulation."[34] From this point of view, the phenomenon of imperialism needs to be examined on the basis of the structural dynamics of the world economy which, in a sense, refers to the internationalization of capitalist production, the process of capitalist accumulation on a world scale, and international capital movements.[35]

As an analytical framework, the theory of the internationalization of capital has been elaborated most fully by Christian Palloix.[36] Palloix's approach is quite unique in that it analyzes the internationalization of capital by utilizing Marx's circuits of capital as presented in volume two of *Das Kapital*. In this context, Palloix's main argument is that the emergence of the multinational corporation—a topic that has recently received much attention by both Marxist and non-Marxist scholars alike—cannot be analyzed at the firm level but, rather, in terms of the structural process of the internationalization of production and capital, and the class struggle on the international scale.[37]

As noted above, Palloix's methodological approach to the question of the internationalization of capital is characterized by its emphasis on the internationalization of the capital accumulation process through the three circuits of capital: the circuit of money-capital ($M....M'$), the circuit of productive-capital ($P....P'$), and the circuit of commodity-capital ($C....C'$). The formula in Figure 4.1 represents the unity of these three circuits and, thus, the self-expansion of social capital.

The concept of social capital refers here "to the self-expansion of industrial capital in the most general and most abstract sense, before its differentiation into specific industrial capitals."[38] Ac-

Figure 4.1
The Circuit of Social Capital

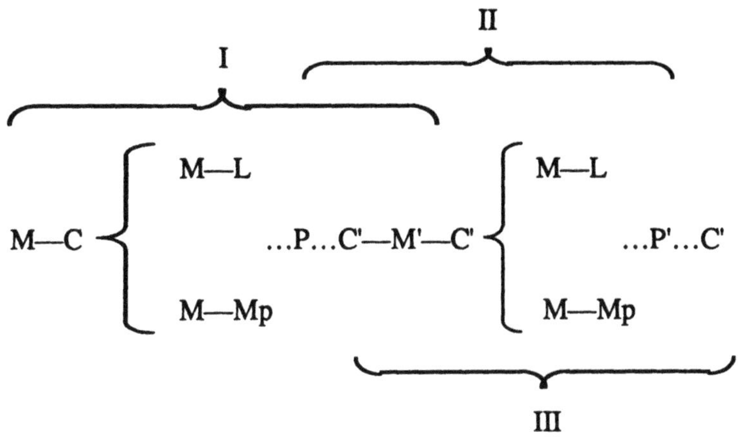

M = money
C = commodities
L = labor-power
Mp = means of production
P = production

Source: Christian Palloix, "The Self-Expansion of Capital on a World Scale," *The Review of Radical Political Economics* 9, no. 2 (Summer 1977), p. 19.

cordingly, the self-expansion of social capital is distinguished from the self-expansion of individual capital precisely because, according to Palloix, "it relies on an *additional* form of capital."[39] As such, Palloix further notes, "even though the self-expansion of individual capital *M-C-M' presupposes* the commodity, the self-expansion of social capital *hinges* on the category of the *commodity*, the central category of the transformation process."[40] The process of the self-expansion of capital is impossible without the commodity form.

From Palloix's perspective, the internationalization of the self-expansion of social capital is essentially the result of the commodity form that is no longer produced in one country. According to him, "this new characteristic means that *commodities* exist—are conceived, produced, and realized—more and more only at the level of the world market and not within the advanced capitalist social formations."[41]

The internationalization of capital is largely a result of the universality of the capitalist mode of production, that is, the generalization of wage labor, the national division, and the law of uneven development. But "the internationalization of capital and the workings of the internal national economy are not antagonistic . . . but are two phenomena which constantly mirror each other."[42] Palloix, however, points out that the internationalization of capital is antagonistic to the struggle of the international working-class movement.[43]

Historically, each stage of capital corresponds to a circuit of capital. However, each circuit of capital "reflects different aspects and different moments"[44] of the self-expansion of capital. Hence international trade, which requires the existence of commodity production on a world scale, can take place without the full introduction of capitalist relations of production.[45] As Clawson points out, "it is therefore not surprising that the circuit of commodity capital was internationalized long before the other circuits."[46] In other words, the internationalization of commodity capital occurs in the first stage.

The transition to capitalism occurs when the circuit of money-capital is internationalized, that is, in the second stage. The second stage "coincides with Lenin's conception of imperialism."[47]

The third stage, which refers to the internationalization of productive-capital, is a contemporary phenomenon, and signifies the expansion of capitalist relations of production on a world scale. This process breaks down all pre-capitalist modes of production and "accelerates the tendency toward industrialization in the Third World."[48] In this context the theory of the internationalization of capital can be viewed as the Marxist theory of development.

SUMMARY AND CONCLUSION

In this chapter we have addressed some of the recent trends among a new generation of Marxist scholarship on the question of imperialism. The modes of production approach and the theory of the internationalization of capital stand out as the most important contributions in the field. Both of them are characterized by their efforts to offer a body of theory that is firmly grounded in the method of classical Marxism. The modes of production approach focuses on the articulation of class relations, while the internationalization of capital offers a framework of analysis that examines the expansion of capital on a global scale and its impact on the growth of the world economy. As such, they represent a major improvement over theories of underdevelopment by virtue of the fact that they are based on an analysis of the dynamics of the capitalist mode of production. However, both approaches have yet to be developed fully. But more important, perhaps, they both contain inherent limitations which, if not overcome, will prevent them from providing with some measurable degree of success a concrete and systematic analysis of the dynamics and contradictions of capitalist imperialism.

Neither the modes of production approach nor the internationalization of capital are based on concrete analyses. In other words, they operate almost exclusively on a highly abstract and theoretical level of analysis. Those employing the modes of production approach, for example, must at some point go beyond theoretical discussions about what constitutes a mode of production and a social formation. It is also of the utmost importance to raise the question of how one would proceed to apply this method of analysis on concrete cases of investigation. In addition to this, the modes of production approach will remain limited in its explanatory value if it continues to detach internal factors from developments in the world capitalist system. The world capitalist system is a reality. International developments have a significant impact within domestic societies. No Marxist theory of imperialism can afford to neglect analyzing international economic relations.

With regard to the internationalization of capital, this particular method of analysis is in the early stages of its theoretical development and articulation. But it does seem to offer a promising way for a serious investigation into the nature of contemporary world economic phenomena and social processes. An analysis of the dynamics of the accumulation of capital on a global scale through an investigation of changes in the structure of the capitalist mode of production has been desperately missing from contemporary Marxist studies on imperialism. The strength and success of Lenin's theory of imperialism (which, in my view, has yet to be duplicated) was derived precisely from the adoption and utilization of such a theoretical model. Moreover, it should also be noted that the internationalization of capital can be used to complement the modes of production approach, since both of them seek to construe an overall perspective of the nature, dynamics, and contradictions of the capitalist mode of production. Perhaps the real theoretical project of Marxist scholarship on imperialism rests with the merging of these two frameworks.

A Marxist theory of imperialism should strive to provide a comprehensive view of the nature of imperialism and its impact on different regions of the world. Far more significantly, the Marxist agenda on scholarship should be shaped by questions pertaining to the dynamics and contradictory relationship between capital and classes, the new structural conditions in the world capitalist economy, and the factors or tendencies that have prevented the collapse of the system of world capitalism. As things stand, neither the modes of production approach nor the internationalization of capital seem to possess all the necessary methodological guidelines for accomplishing these tasks. At best, they can offer broad generalizations and conclusions.

NOTES

1. Bill Warren, "Imperialism and Capitalist Industrialization," *New Left Review*, no. 81 (September-October 1973): 3–44.
2. Ibid., p. 6.
3. Ibid., p. 7.
4. Ibid., p. 7.
5. See Aijaz Ahmad, "Imperialism and Progress," in *Theories of Development: Mode of Production or Dependency?*, Ronald H. Chilcote and Dale L. Johnson (Beverly Hills, CA: Sage Publications, 1983), p. 44.
6. Ibid., p. 45.
7. The difficulty that the case of Korea presents to the neo-Marxist dependency approach is discussed in Aidan Foster-Carter, "Korea and Dependency Theory," *Monthly Review* 37, no. 5 (October 1985): 27–32.
8. Jay R. Mandle, "Marxist Analyses and Capitalist Development in the Third World," *Theory and Society* 9, no. 6 (November 1980): 874.
9. See Bill Warren, "Imperialism and Capitalist Industrialization," pp. 10–16.
10. Ibid., p. 12.
11. Bill Warren, *Imperialism: The Pioneer of Capitalism* (London: New Left Books, 1980).
12. See ibid., pp. 48–83.
13. Ibid., p. 41.
14. Ibid., p. 39.
15. Ibid., p. 41.
16. See Philip McMichael, James Petras, and Robert Rhodes, "Imperialism and the Contradictions of Development," *New Left Review*, no. 85 (May-June 1974): 87.
17. Bill Warren, "Imperialism and Capitalist Industrialization," p. 44.
18. See Karl Marx, *Capital*, vol. 3 (New York: International Publishers, 1967), p. 332.
19. See Louis Althusser and Etienne Balibar, *Reading Capital* (London: Verso, 1979), especially part III, written by Balibar, which sketches a general theory of history based on the concepts of historical materialism. However, it should be pointed out here that much confusion exists about the actual meaning of the term "articulation" as employed by Althusser and Balibar. For a brief discussion on this, see Aidan Foster-Carter, "The Modes of Production Controversy," *New Left Review*, no. 107 (January-February 1978): 52–53.
20. Harold Wolpe, "Introduction," in *The Articulation of Modes of Production*, ed. Harold Wolpe (London: Routledge & Kegan Paul, 1980), pp. 7–8.
21. Louis Althusser and Etienne Balibar, *Reading Capital*, p. 215.

22. Harold Wolpe, "Introduction," in *The Articulation of Modes of Production*, p. 8.

23. Louis Althusser and Etienne Balibar, *Reading Capital*, p. 259.

24. One of the most devastating criticisms launched against Balibar's conception of the mode of production can be found in Barry Hindess and Paul Hirst, *Pre-Capitalist Modes of Production* (London: Routledge & Kegan Paul, 1975), chapter 8.

25. Ernesto Laclau, "Feudalism and Capitalism in Latin America," in *Politics and Ideology in Marxist Theory*, Ernesto Laclau (London: New Left Books, 1977), p. 34.

26. Ibid., pp. 34–35.

27. Pierre-Philippe Rey's major works are *Colonialism, neo-colonialisme et transition au capitalisme* (Paris: Maspero, 1971); and *Les Alliances de classes* (Paris: Maspero, 1973). Our discussion here of the basic ideas in Rey's work is based on the review and analysis provided by Aidan Foster-Carter in "The Modes of Production Controversy," and by Barbara Bradby, "The Destruction of Natural Economy," in *The Articulation of Modes of Production*, ed. Harold Wolpe.

28. Barbara Bradby, "The Destruction of Natural Economy," p. 108.

29. See Harold Wolpe, "The Articulation of Modes and Forms of Production," in *Marxian Theory and the Third World*, ed. Diptendra Banerjee (New Delhi: Sage Publications India, 1985), p. 92.

30. Aidan Foster-Carter, "The Modes of Production Controversy," p. 60.

31. See ibid., pp. 60–62.

32. See Andrew Davidson, "Mode of Production: Impasse or Passe?," *Journal of Contemporary Asia* 19, no. 3 (1989): 245.

33. Magnus Blomstrom and Bjorn Hettne, *Development Theory in Transition* (London: Zed Press, 1984), p. 182.

34. David Barkin, "Internationalization of Capital: An Alternative Approach," *Latin American Perspectives* 8, nos. 3, 4 (Summer and Fall 1981), p. 156.

35. This is the focus of Stephen Hymer's seminal essay "The Internationalization of Capital," *Journal of Economic Issues* 6, no. 1 (March 1972), pp. 91–110.

36. See Christian Palloix, "The Self-Expansion of Capital on a World Scale," *The Review of Radical Political Economics* 9, no. 2 (Summer 1977), pp. 1–28. This article is a translation of Chapter 2 and Appendix 1 from Palloix's book, *L'internationalisation du capital* (Paris: Maspero, 1975).

37. Ibid., p. 4.

38. Ibid., p. 19.

39. Ibid., p. 19.

40. Ibid., p. 19.

41. Ibid., p. 20.
42. Ibid., p. 23.
43. Ibid., p. 23.
44. Patrick Clawson, "The Internationalization of Capital and Capital Accumulation in Iran and Iraq," *The Insurgent Sociologist* 7, no. 2 (Spring 1977), p. 65.
45. Ibid.
46. Ibid.
47. Charles A. Barone, *Marxist Thought on Imperialism: Survey and Critique* (Armonk, NY: M. E. Sharpe, 1985), p. 183.
48. Ibid., p. 183.

Conclusion

The internationalization of capitalist economic life is a socio-economic development that has shaped the reality of the twentieth century. It is hardly possible to imagine any other phenomenon that has had such an impact on the course of social evolution as the changes in the development of capitalism. The dynamics of the structure of the capitalist mode of production, which were analyzed so brilliantly by Marx, have accelerated economic and technological development, and have produced an "inter-dependent" world that is becoming increasingly widespread. Capitalist expansion has led to the creation of a complex, interreacting world economy, reflected in the effort to create the necessary conditions for the constant accumulation of capital. In this way the internationalization of capital has strengthened the system of capitalism by assuring the reproduction of social capital on an international level.

The realization of the internationalization of capitalist economic life, however, has also led to the intensification of the contradictions of the capitalist mode of production. Capitalist integration has paved the way for wholesale crises in the world capitalist system. The first half of the twentieth century saw the results of contradictions among imperialist capitals unfolding in the form of two world wars and a worldwide depression in the 1930s. It also witnessed the world-historic process of socialist revolutions and, especially since World War II, the rise of anti-imperialist struggles in the Third World. These events were produced largely as a result of the law of the uneven economic development of capitalism.

The causes, effects, and contradictions of capitalist imperialism have received extensive treatment by writers operating from within the Marxist intellectual tradition. The major Marxist theoretical figures of early twentieth century devoted considerable attention to the theme of imperialism. Following closely Marx's method and logic of analysis, they produced unique analyses which served as a guide to the struggle of the international working-class movement against imperialism. Lenin's analysis, in particular, disclosed in a highly systematic way the causes and effects of the concentration and centralization of capital and the rise of monopolies. Indeed, the early Marxist theoreticians managed to analyze and explain with great success the development of European capitalism.

In the post-World War II period, the internationalization of capital made gigantic strides under the aegis of U.S. capital. There can be no question that the preponderance of U.S. international economic power led to the restoration of the European capitalist economies and the creation of an economically integrated world. Consequently, the advanced capitalist countries experienced an unprecedented level of economic growth and development during the first twenty or so years since the end of World War II. More significantly, the configuration of the postwar world economy became inextricably intertwined with trans- or supranational structures. Multinational corporations, in particular, penetrated all regions of the world. Nevertheless, the increasing economic penetration of all regions of the world by the internationalization of capital failed to produce sustained economic growth and development for the countries of the Third World. In this connection a new generation of Marxist scholars appeared who sought to take up where the classical Marxist writers had left off.

However, as this study has shown, unlike their predecessors, the new generation of Marxist scholars focused its line of inquiry almost exclusively on the impact of the advanced capitalist countries on the Third World. This was indeed a very important and necessary undertaking, especially in light of the fact that classical Marxism had paid almost no attention to the non-European world. The central question now was to explain the reasons for the failure of successful capitalist development in the Third World. Classical Marxism stressed that the spread of capitalism on a global scale—a tendency produced by the need of capital to discover new markets and new investment opportunities due to the generation of enormous surpluses of capital within the advanced capitalist countries—would eventually lead to the breakdown of all pre-capitalist modes of production. But the realities of the Third World appeared to contradict this thesis.

The articulation of post-World War II Marxist theorization on imperialism intended to offer viable explanations for the causes of underdevelopment in the Third World. In doing so, however, it was soon evident that these analyses were produced in a fashion that displayed little, if any, resemblance to the methodological principles of Marxian political economy. The method of historical materialism was replaced by idealism. Postwar Marxist writers ignored in their analyses the sphere of the relations of production and classes. The contradiction of socialized production and private appropriation disappeared altogether from their analytical framework. The structure of the capitalist mode of production as the theoretical unit of analysis was replaced in turn by an emphasis on the dynamics of the world market. In other words, the sphere of relations of exchange and dependent relationships between the advanced capitalist countries and the so-called periphery formed the conceptual basis of postwar Marxist thought on imperialism. Indeed, they were marked by what might be described as the "fetishism of exchange." Conceiving, thinking, and analyzing international political economy from such an angle, the new generation of Marxist scholars presupposed that imperialism meant merely a process of exploitation and, within this context, that capitalism was a regressive social force that blocked economic development. The new orthodoxy now held that the reason for the increasing gap in economic and social development between the capitalist West and the Third World was due to the form of exploitation imposed by the former on the latter. Both the dependency approach and world-systems theory (which is merely an extension or a derivation from the former) stressed and encouraged the belief (shared by many Third World "radical" leaders) that the incorporation of the "periphery" into the world capitalist system caused development for the capitalist West but underdevelopment for the Third World.

As a result of these shifts in theoretical outlook, Marxism became divided into two distinct schools of thought: classical Marxism and neo-Marxism. The latter school argued that, while its analyses of contemporary imperialism remained essentially within the tradition of Marxist thought, the qualitative new changes in the world capitalist economy necessitated a shift into new lines of thinking. This meant the adoption of methodological procedures that sought to go beyond those employed by classical Marxism. The Labor Theory of Value, and subsequently, the concept of surplus value, was rejected in favor of the bourgeois term "economic surplus." Within this context, capitalism was defined by the advocates of the dependency/world-systems theory approach not as a mode of production but as a world system whose primary function was the pursuit of profit. As a result, neo-Marxists claimed that the spread of trade and capital from Western Europe into the Third World—a process which originated in the late fifteenth century—was an indication that the economies of the Third World had always been capitalistic. Hence underdevelopment was linked to the dynamics and contradictions of the dependent relationship between the advanced capitalist countries and the Third World, or, to those of the world capitalist system as a whole. Thus underdevelopment had nothing to do with the level of development of the productive forces in the Third World. This line of thinking can be encountered in the writings of virtually every major neo-Marxist thinker—from Paul Baran to Arghiri Emmanuel and Samir Amin.

This study has sought to demonstrate that the tenets of neo-Marxism have nothing in common with those of classical Marxism. Indeed the contention here has been that neo-Marxism rests on a set of methodological assumptions that constitutes a clear departure from the method of analysis of historical materialism. Consequently, neo-Marxist analyses of imperialism should not be viewed as part of the Marxist intellectual tradition at all. They form a new, separate theoretical tradition. In addition, the analyses produced by neo-Marxist writers have been incapable of dealing effectively with the causes and effects of imperialism. As this study has pointed out, neo-Marxists analyses are characterized by the tendency to ignore the stages of development in capitalism, thereby confusing capitalist expansion and imperialism. On the other hand, neo-Marxist theorization on the problems of underdevelopment provided no meaningful insights into the causes of this phenomenon. It merely pointed out the consequences of underdevelopment.

In recent years, a new generation of Marxist scholarship has emerged with the aim of analyzing imperialism from a methodological perspective that is closer to the logic of classical Marxism. In particular, the modes of production approach and the theory of the internationalization of capital have moved in directions opposite to that of the dependency/world-systems approach by focusing their attention on the structure of the capitalist mode of production. As such, both of these alternative frameworks possess considerable merit and, even though they have yet to be fully developed, have the potential of establishing the foundation for the realization of a unified Marxist theory of imperialism. In any case, one thing seems certain: the era of domination of neo-Marxist thought on imperialism has passed. Traditional or "orthodox" Marxism is reasserting itself as the new paradigmatic approach in international political economy. But only time will tell as to whether the theoretical and empirical work of the new generation of "orthodox" Marxists will encounter the same success as that attained by the early Marxist theoreticians.

Bibliography

Abdel-Malek, Anouar. *Nation and Revolution*. Albany, NY: State University of New York Press, 1981.

Ahmad, Aijaz. "Imperialism and Progress." In *Theories of Development: Mode of Production or Dependency?*, edited by Ronald H. Chilcote and Dale L. Johnson. Beverly Hills, CA: Sage Publications, 1983.

Alavi, Hamza. "India and the Colonial Mode of Production." In *Socialist Register*, edited by Ralph Miliband and John Saville. London: The Merlin Press, 1975.

Althusser, Louis, and Etienne Balibar. *Reading Capital*. London: Verso, 1979.

Amin, Samir. *Accumulation on a World Scale*. 2 vols. New York: Monthly Review Press, 1974.

______. *Unequal Development: An Essay on the Social Formations of Peripheral Capitalism*. New York: Monthly Review Press, 1976.

______. *The Law of Value and Historical Materialism*. New York: Monthly Review Press, 1978.

______. *Class and Nation: Historically and in the Current Crisis*. New York: Monthly Review Press, 1980.

______. "Modes of Production: History and Unequal Development." *Science & Society* 49, no. 2 (Summer 1985): 194–207.

______. "Colonialism and the Rise of Capitalism: A Comment." *Science & Society* 54, no. 1 (Spring 1990): 67–72.

______. *Delinking: Towards a Polycentric World*. London: Zed Books, 1990.

Anderson, Perry. *Lineages of the Absolutist State*. London: New Left Books, 1979.

Aronowitz, Stanley. "A Metaphysical Critique of Immanuel Wallerstein's The Modern World System." *Theory and Society* 10, no. 4 (July 1981): 503–520.

Arrighi, Giovanni. *The Geometry of Imperialism: The Limits of Hobson's Paradigm*. London: New Left Books, 1978.

Avineri, Shlomo, ed. *Karl Marx on Colonialism and Modernization*. New York: Doubleday, 1968.

Baechler, Jean, Michael Mann, and John A. Hall, eds. *Europe and the Rise of Capitalism*. London: Oxford University Press, 1987.

Bailey, Anne M., and Josep R. Llobera, eds. *The Asiatic Mode of Production: Science and Politics*. London: Routledge and Kegan Paul, 1981.

Banerjee, Diptendra, ed. *Marxian Theory and the Third World*. New Delhi: Sage Publications India, 1985.

Baran, Paul. *The Political Economy of Growth*. New York: Monthly Review Press, 1957.

______. *The Longer View: Essays Toward a Critique of Political Economy*. New York: Monthly Review Press, 1969.

Baran, Paul, and Paul M. Sweezy. *Monopoly Capital*. New York: Monthly Review Press, 1966.

Barclay, William, and Mitchell Stengel. "Surplus and Surplus-Value." *Review of Radical Political Economics* 7, no. 4 (Winter 1975): 48–64.

Barkin, David. "Internationalization of Capital: An Alternative Approach." *Latin American Perspectives* 8, nos. 3, 4 (Summer and Fall 1981): 156–160.

Barone, Charles A. *Marxist Thought on Imperialism: Survey and Critique*. Armonk, NY: M. E. Sharpe, 1985.

Becker, James F. *Marxian Political Economy*. Cambridge: Cambridge University Press, 1977.

Berberoglu, Berch. "The Controversy Over Imperialism and Capitalist Industrialization: Critical Notes on the Dependence Theory." *Journal of Contemporary Asia* 4, no. 4 (1984): pp. 399–407.

______. *The Internationalization of Capital*. New York: Praeger Publishers, 1987.

Berki, R. N. "On Marxian Thought and the Problem of International Relations." *World Politics* 24, no. 1 (1971): pp. 80–105.

Berlin, Isaiah. *Karl Marx: His Life and Environment*. New York: Oxford University Press, 1963.

Bienefeld, Manfred. "The Lessons of History and the Developing World." *Monthly Review* 41, no. 3 (July-August 1989): 9–41.

Blaut, J. M. "Colonialism and the Rise of Capitalism." *Science & Society* 53, no. 3 (Fall 1989): 260–296.

Bleaney, M. F. *UnderConsumption Theories: A History and Critical Analysis*. New York: International Publishers, 1976.

Blomstrom, Magnus, and Bjorn Hettne. *Development Theory in Transition*. London: Zed Books, 1984.

Boulding, Kenneth, and Tapan Mukerjee, eds. *Economic Imperialism*. Ann Arbor: University of Michigan Press, 1972.

Bradby, Barbara. "The Destruction of Natural Economy." In *The Articulation of Modes of Production*, edited by Harold Wolpe. London: Routledge and Kegan Paul, 1980.

Braudel, Fernand. *The Structures of Everyday Life*. New York: Harper & Row, 1979.

______. *The Wheels of Commerce*. New York: Harper & Row, 1983.

______. *The Perspective of the World*. New York: Harper & Row, 1984.

Brenner, Robert. "The Origins of Capitalist Development: A Critique of Neo-Smithian Marxism." *New Left Review*, no. 104 (July-August 1977): 25–92.

Brewer, Anthony. *Marxist Theories of Imperialism*: A Critical Survey. London: Routledge and Kegan Paul, 1980.

Brown, Michael Barratt. *After Imperialism*. London: Heinemann, 1970.

______. "A Critique of Marxist Theories of Imperialism." In *Studies in the Theory of Imperialism*, edited by Roger Owen and Bob Sutcliffe. London: Longman, 1972.

______. *The Economics of Imperialism*. Baltimore: Penguin Books, 1974.

Brutens, K. N. *National Revolutions Today*. Parts 1 and 2. Moscow: Progress Publishers, 1977.

Bukharin, Nikolai. *Imperialism and World Economy*. New York: Howard Fertig, 1966.

______. *Imperialism and the Accumulation of Capital*. New York: Monthly Review Press, 1972.

______. *Historical Materialism: A System of Sociology*. Ann Arbor: The University of Michigan Press, 1976.

Callinicos, Alex. *Making History*. Ithaca, NY: Cornell University Press, 1988.

Cameron, Kenneth Neill. *Marxism: The Science of Society*. South Hadley, MA: Bergin & Garvey Publishers, 1985.

Carchedi, Guglielmo. "Emmanuel's 'Narrow' Unequal Exchange." *International Journal of Political Economy* 18, no. 3 (Fall 1988): 53–58.

Cardoso, Fernando Henrique. "Dependency and Development in Latin America." *New Left Review*, no. 74 (July-August 1972): 83–95.

Cardoso, Fernando Henrique, and Enso Faletto. *Dependency and Development in Latin America*. Berkeley: University of California Press, 1979.

Catephores, George. *An Introduction to Marxist Economics*. New York: New York University Press, 1989.

Chilcote, Ronald H. "Dependency: A Critical Synthesis of the Literature." *Latin American Perspectives* 1, no. 1 (Spring 1974): 4–29.

______. "A Question of Dependency." *Latin American Research Review* 13, no. 2 (1978): 55–68.

______. *Theories of Development and Underdevelopment*. Boulder, CO: Westview Press, 1984.

Clawson, Patrick. "The Internationalization of Capital and Capital Accumulation in Iran and Iraq." *The Insurgent Sociologist* 7, no. 2 (Spring 1977): 64–73.

Cohen, Benjamin. *The Question of Imperialism*. New York: Basic Books, 1973.

Cohen, G. A. *Karl Marx's Theory of History: A Defense*. Oxford: Clarendon Press, 1978.

Colletti, Lucio. *From Rousseau to Lenin: Studies in Ideology and Society*. New York: Monthly Review Press, 1974.

Cypher, James. "The Internationalization of Capital and the Transformation of Social Formations: A Critique of the Monthly Review School." *Review of Radical Political Economics* 11, no. 4 (Winter 1979): 33–49.

Davidson, Andrew. "Mode of Production: Impasse or Passe?" *Journal of Contemporary Asia* 19, no. 3 (1989): 243–278.

Desai, Meghnad. *Marxian Economic Theory*. London: Gray-Mills Publishing Ltd., 1974.

Dobb, Maurice. *Studies in the Development of Capitalism*. London: Routledge and Kegan Paul, 1963.

Dupuy, Alex, and Paul V. Fitzgerald. "A Contribution to the Critique of the World System Perspective." *The Insurgent Sociologist* 7, no. 2 (Spring 1977): 113–124.

Emmanuel, Arghiri. *Unequal Exchange: A Study of the Imperialism of Trade*. New York: Monthly Review Press, 1972.

______. "Myths of Development Versus Myths of Underdevelopment." *New Left Review*, no. 85 (June 1974): 61–82.

Etherington, Norman. *Theories of Imperialism: War, Conquest, and Capital*. London: Croom Helm, 1984.

Fernandez, Paul A., and Jose F. Ocampo. "The Latin American Revolution: A Theory of Imperialism, Not Dependence." *Latin American Perspectives* 1, no. 1 (Spring 1974): 30–61.

Fine, Ben. "On the Origins of Capitalist Development." *New Left Review*, no. 109 (May-June 1978): 88–95.

Fine, Ben, and Lawrence Harris. *Rereading Capital*. London: Macmillan, 1979.

Foster-Carter, Aidan. "The Modes of Production Controversy," *New Left Review*, no. 107 (January-February 1978): 47–77.

______. "Korea and Dependency Theory." *Monthly Review* 37, no. 5 (October 1985): 27–34.

Foster, John Bellamy. *The Theory of Monopoly Capitalism: An Elaboration of Marxian Political Economy*. New York: Monthly Review Press, 1986.

Frank, Andre Gunder. *Capitalism and Underdevelopment in Latin America*. New York: Monthly Review Press, 1967.

______. "The Development of Underdevelopment." In *Latin America: Underdevelopment or Revolution*? New York: Monthly Review Press, 1969.

______. *Lumpenbourgeoisie and Lumpendevelopment: Dependency, Class and Politics in Latin America*. New York: Monthly Review Press, 1972.

______. *World Accumulation, 1492–1789*. New York: Monthly Review Press, 1978.

______. *Dependent Accumulation and Underdevelopment*. New York Monthly Review Press, 1979.

______. *Crisis: In the World Economy*. New York: Holmes and Meier, 1980.

______. *Crisis: In the Third World*. New York: Holmes and Meier, 1981.

Furtado, Celso. *Development and Underdevelopment*. Berkeley: University of California Press, 1964.

______. "The Concept of External Dependence in the Study of Underdevelopment." In *The Political Economy of Development and Underdevelopment*, edited by Charles K. Wilder. New York: Random House, 1973.

Garaudy, Roger. *Karl Marx: The Evolution of His Thought*. Reprint. Westport, CT: Greenwood Press, 1976.

Garst, Daniel. "Wallerstein and His Critics." *Theory and Society* 14, no. 4 (July 1985): 469–495.

Gerstein, Ira. "Theories of the World Economy and Imperialism." *The Insurgent Sociologist* 7, no. 2 (Spring 1977): 9–22.

Gorin, Zeev. "Socialist Societies and World System Theory: A Critical Survey." *Science & Society* 49, no. 3 (Fall 1985): 332–366.

Harvey, David. *The Limits to Capital*. Chicago: The University of Chicago Press, 1982.

Hilferding, Rudolf. *Finance Capital*. London: Routledge and Kegan Paul, 1981.

Hindess, Barry, and Paul Hirst. *Pre-Capitalist Modes of Production*. London: Routledge and Kegan Paul, 1975.

Hobsbawm, Eric. "Marx and History." *New Left Review*, no. 143 (January-February 1984): 39–50.

Hobson, John Atkinson. *Imperialism: A Study*. London: George Allen and Unwin, 1954.

Holton, Robert J. "Marxist Theories of Social Change and the Transition from Feudalism to Capitalism." *Theory and Society* 10, no. 6 (November 1981): 833–867.

Howard, M. C., and J. E. King. *A History of Marxian Economics, Vol. 1, 1883–1929*. Princeton: Princeton University Press, 1989.

Hymer, Stephen. "The Internationalization of Capital." *Journal of Economic Issues* 6, no. 1 (March 1972): 91–111.

Jessop, Bob. *The Capitalist State: Marxist Theories and Methods*. New York: New York University Press, 1982.

Johnson, Carlos. "Ideologies in Theories of Imperialism and Dependency." In *Theories of Development: Mode of Production or Dependency?* edited by Ronald H. Chilcote and Dale L. Johnson. Beverly Hills, CA: Sage Publications, 1983.

Kakonen, Jyrki. *Natural Resources and Conflicts in the Changing International System: Three Studies on Imperialism*. Aldershot, England: Gower Publishing Co., 1988.

Katz, Claudio J. *From Feudalism to Capitalism: Marxian Theories of Class Struggle and Social Change*. Westport, CT: Greenwood Press, 1989.

Kay, Geoffrey. *Development and Underdevelopment: A Marxist Analysis*. London: Macmillan, 1975.

Kemp, Tom. *Theories of Imperialism*. London: Dobson Books, 1967.

Kiernan, V. G. *Marxism and Imperialism*. London: Edward Arnold, 1974.

Kolko, Joyce. *Restructuring the World Economy*. New York: Pantheon Books, 1988.

Kostopoulos, Tryphon. *Beyond Capitalism Toward Nomocracy*. New York: Praeger Publishers, 1986.

Kozlov, G. A. *Political Economy: Capitalism*. Moscow: Progress Publishers, 1977.

Krader, Lawrence. *The Asiatic Mode of Production: Sources, Development, and Critique in the Writings of Karl Marx*. Assen, The Netherlands: Van Gorcum, 1975.

Kühne, Karl. *Economics and Marxism, Vol I: The Renaissance of the Marxian System*. Translated by Robert Shaw. New York: St. Martin's Press, 1979.

______. *Economics and Marxism, Vol II: The Dynamics of the Marxian System*. New York: St. Martin's Press, 1979.

Laclau, Ernesto. "Feudalism and Capitalism in Latin America." *New Left Review*, no. 67, (May/June 1971), reprinted, with postscript, in Ernesto Laclau, *Politics and Ideology in Marxist Theory*. London: New Left Books, 1977.

Laibman, David. "Modes of Production and Theories of Transition." *Science & Society* 48, no. 3 (Fall 1984): 257–294.

Larrain, Jorge. *A Reconstruction of Historical Materialism*. London: Allen and Unwin, 1986.

Leaver, Richard. "The Debate of Underdevelopment: 'On Situating Andre Gunder Frank,' " *Journal of Contemporary Asia* 7, no. 1 (1977): 108–115.

Lenin, V. I. *The Development of Capitalism in Russia*. Moscow: Progress Publishers, 1956.

______. "On the So-Called Market Question." In *Collected Works*, Vol. 1. Moscow: Progress Publishers, 1972.

______. "The Lessons of the Crisis." In *Collected Works*, Vol. 5. Moscow: Progress Publishers, 1972.

______. *Imperialism: The Highest Stage of Capitalism*. In *Selected Works* in one volume. New York: International Publishers, 1976.

Lichtheim, George. *Imperialism*. New York: Praeger Publishers, 1971.

Linklàter, Andrew. *Beyond Realism and Marxism: Critical Theory and International Relations*. New York: St. Martin's Press, 1990.

Lippit, Victor D. "The Concept of the Surplus in Economic Development." *Review of Radical Political Economics*, vol. 17, nos. 1–2 (1985): 1–19.

Loewenstein, Julius I. *Marx Against Marxism*. London: Routledge and Kegan Paul, 1980.

Lotta, Raymond, with Frank Shannon. *America in Decline: An Analysis of the Developments Toward War and Revolution, in the U.S. and Worldwide, in the 1980s*. Vol. 1. Chicago: Banner Press, 1984.

Luxemburg, Rosa. *The Accumulation of Capital*. New Haven, CT: Yale University Press, 1951.

______. *The Accumulation of Capital—An Anti-Critique*. New York: Monthly Review Press, 1972.

Magdoff, Harry. *The Age of Imperialism*. New York: Monthly Review Press, 1969.

Mandel, Ernest. "After Imperialism?" *New Left Review*, no. 25 (May-June 1964): 17–25.

______. "Surplus Value and Realization of Surplus Value." *International Socialist Review* 28, no. 1 (January-February 1967): 56–64.

______. "The Labor Theory of Value and Monopoly Capitalism." *International Socialist Review* 28, no. 4 (July-August 1967): 29–42.

______. *Europe vs. America: Contradictions of Imperialism*. New York: Monthly Review Press, 1970.

______. *Late Capitalism*. London: New Left Books, 1975.

Mandle, Jay R. "Marxist Analyses and Capitalist Development in the Third World." *Theory and Society* 9, no. 6 (November 1980): 865–876.

Mars, Perry. "Political Determinants of Revolutionary Change in the Third World." *Social Praxis* 8, nos. 1–2 (1981): 95–119.

Marx, Karl. *Pre-Capitalist Economic Formations*. Edited by E. J. Hobsbawm. London: Lawrence and Wishart, 1964.

______. *Capital.* 3 vols. New York: International Publishers, 1967.

______. *The Eighteenth Brumaire of Louis Bonaparte*. In *Selected Works* in one volume. New York: International Publishers, 1968.

______. *Theories of Surplus Value*. Vol. 2. London: Lawrence and Wishart, 1969.

______. *A Contribution to the Critique of Political Economy*, edited with introduction by Maurice Dobb. New York: International Publishers, 1970.

______. *Grundrisse*. Translated with a Foreword by Martin Nicolaus. New York: Vintage Books, 1973.

______. *The Poverty of Philosophy*. In *Collected Works*, vol. 6. New York: International Publishers, 1976.

Marx, Karl, and Friedrich Engels. *Selected Correspondence, 1846–1895*. Translated by Dora Torr. Westport, CT: Greenwood Press, 1975.

______. *On Colonialism*. New York: International Publishers, 1972.

______. *The German Ideology*. In *Collected Works*, vol. 5. New York: International Publishers, 1976.

______. *Manifesto of the Communist Party*. In *Collected Works*, vol. 6. New York: International Publishers, 1976.

McLennan, Gregor. *Marxism and the Methodologies of History*. London: New Left Books, 1981.

McMichael, Philip, James Petras, and Robert Rhodes. "Imperialism and the Contradictions of Development." *New Left Review*, no. 85 (May-June 1974): 83–104.

McMurtry, John. *The Structure of Marx's World-View*. Princeton, NJ: Princeton University Press, 1978.

Meiskins, Peter. "Productive and Unproductive Labor in Marx's Theory of Class." *Review of Radical Political Economics* 13, no. 3 (Fall 1981): 32–42.

Miliband, Ralph. "Marx and the State." In *Socialist Register*. London: Merlin Press, 1965.

______. *The State in Capitalist Society*. New York: Basic Books, 1969.

Mittelman, James H. *Out From Underdevelopment: Prospects for the Third World*. New York: St. Martin's Press, 1988.

Mohun, Simon. "Abstract Labor and Its Value-Form." *Science & Society* 48, no. 4 (Winter 1984–85): 388–406.

Mommsen, Wolfgang. *Theories of Imperialism*. New York: Random House, 1980.

Mouzelis, Nicos P. "Sociology of Development: Reflections on the Present Crisis." *Sociology* 22, no. 1 (February 1988): 23–44.

Murray, Robin. "The Internationalization of Capital and the Nation State." *New Left Review*, 67 (May-June 1971): 84–109.

Nabudere, Dan. *The Political Economy of Imperialism*. London: Zed Press, 1977.

Nathan, Otto. "Marxism and Monopoly Capital." *Science & Society* 30, no. 4 (Fall 1966): 487–496.

Navarro, .Vincente. "The Limits of World-Systems Theory." In *Socialist States in the World Economy*, edited by Christopher K. Chase-Dunn. Beverly Hills, CA: Sage Publications, 1982.

Novack, George. *Uneven and Combined Development in History*. New York: Merit Publishers, 1966.

_____. *An Introduction to the Logic of Marxism*. New York: Pathfinder Press, 1971.

Oakley, Allen. *Marx's Critique of Political Economy: Intellectual Sources and Evolution, Vol. I: 1844 to 1860*. London: Routledge and Kegan Paul, 1984.

_____. *Marx's Critique of Political Economy: Intellectual Sources and Evolution, Vol. II: 1861 to 1863*. London: Routledge and Kegan Paul, 1985.

O'Connor, James. "Monopoly Capital." *New Left Review*, no. 40 (November-December 1966): 38–50.

_____. "The Meaning of Economic Imperialism." In *Imperialism and Underdevelopment: A Reader*, edited by Robert I. Rhodes. New York: Monthly Review Press, 1970.

O'Leary, Brendan. *The Asiatic Mode of Production: Oriental Despotism, Historical Materialism, and Indian History*. New York: Basil Blackwell, 1989.

Onimode, Bade. *An Introduction to Marxist Political Economy*. London: Zed Press, 1985.

Ougaard, Morten. "Some Remarks Concerning Peripheral Capitalism and the Peripheral State." *Science & Society* 46, no. 4 (Winter 1982–1983): 385–404.

Owen, Roger, and Bob Sutcliffe, eds. *Studies in the Theory of Imperialism*. London: Longman, 1972.

Pachter, Harry. "The Problem of Imperialism." *Dissent* 17, no. 5 (September-October 1970): 461–488.

Palloix, Christian. *L'internationalisation du capital*. Paris: Maspero, 1975.

_____. "The Internationalization of Capital and the Circuit of Social Capital." In *International Firms and Modern Imperialism*, edited by Hugo Radich. London: Penguin, 1975.

_____. "The Self-Expansion of Capital on a World Scale." *Review of Radical Political Economics* 9, no. 2 (Summer 1977): 3–28.

Perkins, Katherine M. *Production, Distribution and Growth in Transitional Economies*. New York: Praeger Publishers, 1988.

Petras, James. *Critical Perspectives on Imperialism and Social Class in the Third World*. New York: Monthly Review Press, 1978.

______. *Class, State, and Power in the Third World*. London: Zed Press, 1981.

______. "Dependency and World System Theory: A Critique and New Directions." *Latin American Perspectives* 8, nos. 3 and 4 (Summer and Fall 1981): 148–155.

Petras, James F., and Morris H. Morley. "The Imperial State in the Rise and Fall of U.S. Imperialism." In *Instability and Change in the World Economy*, edited by Arthur MacEwan and William K. Tabb. New York: Monthly Review Press, 1989.

Pieterse, Jan Nederveen. "A Critique of World System Theory." *International Sociology* 3, no. 3 (September 1988): 251–266.

Poulantzas, Nicos. *Political Power and Social Classes*. London: New Left Books, 1973.

______. *Classes in Contemporary Capitalism*. London: New Left Books, 1975.

______. *The Review of Radical Political Economics* 5, no. 1 (Spring 1973). Special Issue: "Capitalism and World Economic Integration: Perspectives on Modern Imperialism."

Rey, Pierre-Philippe. *Colonialism, neo-colonialisme et transition au capitalisme*. Paris: Maspero, 1971.

______. *Les Alliances de classes*. Paris: Maspero, 1973.

Rowthorn, Bob. "Imperialism in the Seventies—Unity or Rivalry?" *New Left Review*, no. 69 (September-October 1971): 31–54.

Sau, Ranjit. *Unequal Exchange, Imperialism and Underdevelopment*. Calcutta: Oxford University Press, 1978.

Sawer, Marian. *Marxism and the Question of the Asiatic Mode of Production*. The Hague: Martinus Nijhoff, 1977.

Sayer, Derek. *Marx's Method: Ideology, Science and Critique in Capital*. Hassocks, England: Harvester Press, 1979.

______. *The Violence of Abstraction: The Analytic Foundations of Historical Materialism*. New York: Basil Blackwell, 1987.

Schmidt, Alfred. *History and Structure: An Essay on Hegelian-Marxist and Structuralist Theories of History*. Cambridge, MA: The MIT Press, 1983.

Schmitt, Richard. "The Materialist Dialectic." *Science & Society* 52, no. 4 (Winter 1988): 441–456.

Shanin, Teodor, ed. *Late Marx and the Russian Road: Marx and the Peripheries of Capitalism*. London: Routledge and Kegan Paul, 1983.

Shaw, William H. *Marx's Theory of History*. Stanford, CA: Stanford University Press, 1978.

Skocpol, Theda. "Wallerstein's World Capitalist System: A Theoretical and Historical Critique." *American Journal of Sociology* 82, no. 5 (March 1977): 1075–1090.

Stanfield, Ron. "A Revision of the Economic Surplus Concept." *Review of Radical Political Economics* 6, no. 3 (Fall 1974): 69–74.

Stavrianos, L. S. *Global Rift: The Third World Comes of Age*. New York: William Morrow, 1981.

Sweezy, Paul. *The Theory of Capitalist Development*. New York: Monthly Review Press, 1968.

______. "On the Theory of Monopoly Capitalism." *Monthly Review* 23, no. 11 (April 1972). 1–23.

Sweezy, Paul, and Harry Magdoff. *The Dynamics of U.S. Capitalism*. New York: Monthly Review Press, 1972.

Szentes, Tamas. *The Political Development of Underdevelopment*. Budapest: Akademiai, 1983.

______. *The Transformation of the World Economy*. London: Zed Books, 1988.

Szymanski, Albert. "Capital Accumulation on a World Scale and the Necessity of Imperialism." *The Insurgent Sociologist* 7, no. 2 (Spring 1977): 35–53.

______. *The Logic of Imperialism*. New York: Praeger Publishers, 1981.

Taylor, John. *From Modernization to Modes of Production: A Critique of the Sociologies of Development and Underdevelopment*. London: Macmillan, 1979.

Thomas, Clive Y. "Restructuring of the World Economy and Its Political Implications for the Third World." In *Instability and Change in the World Economy*, edited by Arthur MacEwan and William K. Tabb. New York: Monthly Review Press, 1989.

Tyagunenko, V. L. *Industrialization of Developing Countries*. Moscow: Progress Publishers, 1973.

Varga, Eugen. *Politico-Economic Problems of Capitalism*. Moscow: Progress Publishers, 1968.

Wallerstein, Immanuel. "Dependence in an Interdependent World: Possibilities of Transformation Within the Capitalist World-Economy." *African Studies Review* 17, no. 1 (April 1974): 1–23.

______. *The Modern World-System: Capitalist Agriculture and the Origins of the European World-Economy in the Sixteenth Century*. New York: Academic Press, 1974.

______. "The Rise and Future Demise of the World Capitalist System: Concepts for Comparative Analysis." *Comparative Studies in Society and History* 16, no. 4 (1974): 387–415.

______. *The Capitalist World-Economy*. London: Cambridge University Press, 1979.

______. *The Modern World-System II: Mercantilism and the Consolidation of the European World Economy 1600–1750*. New York: Academic Press, 1980.

______. "The States in the Institutional Vortex of the Capitalist World-Economy." *International Social Science Journal* 32, no. 4 (1980): 743–751.

______. "Imperialism and Development." In *Studies of the Modern World-System*, edited by Albert Bergesen. New York: Academic Press, 1980.

______. *The Modern World-System III: The Second Era of Great Expansion of the Capitalist World-Economy, 1730–1840s*. New York: Academic Press, 1989.

Warren, Bill. "The Internationalization of Capital and the Nation State: A Comment." *New Left Review*, no. 68 (July-August 1971): 83–88.

______. "Imperialism and Capitalist Industrialization." *New Left Review*, no. 81 (September-October 1973): 3–44.

______. *Imperialism: Pioneer of Capitalism*. London: New Left Books, 1980.

Weeks, John. "The Sphere of Production and the Analysis of Crisis in Capitalism," *Science & Society* 41, no. 3 (Fall 1977): 281–302.

______. *Capital and Exploitation*. Princeton: Princeton University Press, 1981.

Weeks, John, and Elizabeth Dore. "International Exchange and the Causes of Backwardness." *Latin American Perspectives* 6, no. 2 (Spring 1979): 62–87.

Weisskopf, Thomas. "Capitalism, Underdevelopment and the Future of the Poor Countries." *Review of Radical Political Economics* 4, no. 1 (Winter 1972): 1–35.

______. "Theories of American Imperialism: A Critical Evaluation." *Review of Radical Political Economics* 6, no. 3 (Fall 1974): 41–60.

Willoughby, John. *Capitalist Imperialism, Crisis and the State*. London: Harwood Academic Publishers, 1986.

Wolpe, Harold, ed. *The Articulation of Modes of Production*. London: Routledge and Kegan Paul, 1980.

Wood, Ellen Meiskins. "Marxism and the Course of History." *New Left Review*, no. 147 (September-October 1984): 95–107.

Worsley, Peter. "One World or Three? A Critique of the World-System Theory of Immanuel Wallerstein." In *States and Societies*, edited by David Held et al. New York: New York University Press, 1983.

Index

ABOUT THE AUTHOR

CHRONIS POLYCHRONIOU, born in Athens, Greece, is an assistant professor of political science at Lincoln University, Pennsylvania, where he has been teaching since 1986.

Polychroniou studied philosophy at Temple University, American studies (with specialization in American foreign policy) at Saint Joseph's University in Philadelphia, and political science at the University of Delaware.

His areas of focus are international relations, international political economy, and political theory. Currently Polychroniou is working on his next book, which deals with the international political history of Marxism and the future of socialism.

www.ingramcontent.com/pod-product-compliance
Ingram Content Group UK Ltd.
Pitfield, Milton Keynes, MK11 3LW, UK
UKHW020207290926
15470UKWH00001B/44